# I AM
# MARRIED
# BUT LONELY:
# WHY?

*Issues in Marital Loneliness and Intimacy*

## CORNELIUS UCHE OKEKE

# DEDICATION

**This book is dedicated to all married men and women who have not given up in their struggle with marital loneliness**

# Foreword

We often times hear people say that they are alone or that they are lonely. Often times, too, people tend to confuse being alone with being lonely. It is doubtful if any writer around us has taken pains to venture into marital loneliness as a subject or topic. The focus has always been on being alone, for being lonely, which terms are quite distinct from one another. Consequently, marital loneliness has not really been given attention and little or no efforts have been made to consider the causes and consequences of this cankerworm that has been eating deep into the foundation of very many marital relationships.

The author of this book, Fr. Cornelius Okeke, has taken great pains to x-ray the various aspects of loneliness including being alone. He has dealt extensively and exhaustively on the causes and consequences of marital loneliness including spiritual and social loneliness. He also reviewed all the relevant issues that culminate in marital loneliness – lack of affection, falsehood, class distinction, economic stratification, social stigmatization, family influences, cultural and traditional beliefs and practices, the psyche of the persons involved in marital relationships and many more. Sequel to these issues, are the divergent problems that persons expriencing marital loneliness are confronted with which, oftentimes, have lasting negative consequences on such persons. This aspect of this work will certainly be of immense help and value to all those interested in working towards stabilized marital relationship.

The chapters of this book constitute a systematic and well-structured layout of all that one must know about marital loneliness and thus be in a better position to either guard against it or retrace one's footsteps, if on it. The topics in the various chapters are of vast importance and their treatment shows the highest order of scholarship.

The book is very useful in addition to the growing need for marital stability and I recommend it to parents, youths, priests, religious, laity, the general public, and to all and sundry as a valuable and indispensable guide and/or resource material for the various marital choices made and decisions taken so that anyone that makes such choices and decisions accepts full responsibility for them.

Nwando C. Obiano Esq. Ph.D
5th January, 2007.

# Preface

*What a strange thing is loneliness, and how frightening it is! We never allow ourselves to get too close to it; and if by chance we do, we quickly run away from it. We will do anything to escape from loneliness, to cover it up.*
- J. Krishnamurti

*Loneliness is a taste of death. No wonder some people who are desperately lonely lose themselves in mental illness or violence to forget the inner pain.*
- Jean Vanier

Loneliness is one experience human beings dread. Yet, it is an experience that is universal. In communitarian cultures, loneliness expresses itself more as a feeling of being left out, of not belonging. From childhood, we actively seek and enjoy the company of others; we are scared of being left alone. A child who grows up feeling lonely will certainly have some problems in his or her life. As we grow up, we find ourselves forging healthy and unhealthy relationships with others as long as we are shielded from the pain of loneliness. We struggle for the rest of our lives dealing with the unhealthy and stifling relationships we formed as we grew up. As we mature physically and psychologically, some of us succeed in dropping our unhealthy relationships and maintaining the healthy ones. But there are many people who move from one unhealthy relationship to the other driven by fear of loneliness. In individualistic cultures, persons tend to keep quasi-marital relationships till the end of their lives because it is hard to deal with loneliness.

Loneliness can result from some existential situations such as the loss of a loved one, a beloved spouse, a good friend, separation, leaving one's homeland to a foreign land, rejection or abandonment by a trusted friend, having unsatisfied life and relationships, and so on. The loneliness experienced in these existential conditions is usually expected, and adults and children go through it. Loneliness within marriage is least expected and is usually deep and profound. This should not come as a surprise to anyone because the fear of loneliness is one of the reasons some people get married. In fact, it is a strong subconscious expectation that marriage would take care of the loneliness in their lives. After all, companionship is an important aspect of married life. Unmarried persons and even celibates admire and fantasize about the peaceful bond of marriage that would deal with their experience of loneliness forever. Yet, there are lots of married people who are lonely. It seems a contradiction in terms: to be married and be lonely at the same time.

I did not imagine that such would be possible in our African-Igbo culture where marriage and being a mother or a father top the list of the aspirations of young women and men. These are important cultural values. I was drawn to this problem of loneliness of married persons during counseling sessions and presentations I have given on relationships. Though there is no statistical data to work with, I am sure the percentage of married persons, men and women, in this condition is not low. On one occasion, I was in a seminar on this topic with young unmarried men and women, and I casually asked them whether they would prefer to get married or remain single if there were no social stigmatization of the unmarried state. I was surprised to find out that a good number, mostly women, said they would prefer to remain single if their parents and the society would not frown at them. This aroused my curiosity. I voiced my disbelief, and they told me that I would not understand because I am a Catholic priest. They told me that the stories of their married friends tended to be disappointing. They said they would prefer to remain single and keep their friends. There were some others in the group, however, who were convinced that marriage was their better choice because they would not expect one hundred percent of everything. Those people told stories of their married friends and parents who served as models for them. But this group is the minority.

The idea for this book came from the encounter of that day. I owe those young men and women a lot for providing the inspiration for it. My desire is first, to examine the marital relationship closely and provide some insights that would help those who feel called to the married state to give themselves fully to it, and with joy face the challenges that come therefrom. Secondly, I want also to expand the perspective of our thinking about marriage especially in our African-Igbo culture. Finally, I situate the discussion and reflection of this book in the context of human development, with the conviction that our various vocations in life are avenues to grow and mature in our fundamental human vocation. The overall aim is to widen the horizon of those preparing to get married and those who are already in this problem in order to increase the number of married persons who have encouraging and challenging stories to tell about their married life.

In a general way, I want to thank those who have been giving me support in my efforts to explore some areas of our everyday life. First are my colleagues at the Pope John Paul II Major Seminary, Okpuno-Awka, Anambra State, Nigeria, and my students from whom I get valuable feedbacks after raising some aspects of the work in the class or in discussion. Fr. Eugene Anowai, the Vice Rector of the seminary, devoted his time to read through the manuscript. I remain grateful to him. I thank by bosom friend Fr. Lawrence Nwankwo who brought much of his giftedness into this work in order to improve its quality. He called my attention to certain facts that I either took for granted or expressed in an ambiguous way. I thank him as well as Fr. Tony Umeh who made important suggestions concerning the title. My good friends Dr. Vincent Ofoegbu and his wife Barrister Chinenye, took time to go through the manuscript and offered their invaluable suggestions. I thank them also for commenting about the book. Dr. Nwando Obiano (Esq.), did not hesitate to find time to go through the draft and write the foreword. I am grateful to her. Wanda Edie has always supported me with reading materials as well as Matt and Carol Fett. I thank them immensely. Bill and Margaret Terrien are great persons in my life, and I thank them for all their encouragements. Bill went through the first draft and made important corrections. I appreciate it a lot. Michael Lavigne is a good friend who designed the cover without any charge. I appreciate the time it took him to arrive at the concept that captured the ideas expressed in this book. I remain grateful to him. May the fruits of this work bring blessings in your lives. Amen.

Cornelius Uche Okeke
7th February, 2007.

Cornelius Uche Okeke

# Table of Content

**Pages**

**Dedication**......................................................................iii

**Foreword**.......................................................................v

**Preface**.........................................................................vii

I   Alone or lonely?.........................................................1
    Two major forms of loneliness................................5
    Loneliness: physical and psychological effects.....20
    The pain of being married and lonely....................23
    Summary.....................................................................27

II  Anatomy of marital loneliness...............................28
    Signs and symptoms of marital loneliness............30
    A tragic story of marital loneliness: The Prince
    and Princess of Wales...............................................49

III Why and how married people arrive at loneliness.56
    The shadow side of cultural ideals........................57
    Desires of personality..............................................79
    Summary.....................................................................112

IV  Preparing for marriage...........................................113
    An important question: why do you want to
    marry him or her?......................................................115
    Know the person you want to marry.....................121
    Marriage is for commitment...................................134

V   Beyond having children: Building marital
    Intimacy......................................................................140
    Happily married: the story of intimacy
    and commitment........................................................141
    Meaning and nurturing of intimacy......................145
    Intimacy and sex in marriage................................151

**Notes**..........................................................................**157**

Cornelius Uche Okeke

# I

## ALONE OR LONELY?

*Solitude takes other forms: the desire toward the silence of nature or the solitude of listening to poetry, or reading it, or listening to music, or viewing works of art. At such times we are alone even in the midst of crowds, but we are not lonely.*

Clark E.Moustakas

People often say, "I feel lonely" or "I don't want to be alone". When we hear these expressions, we tend to feel right away that we know what the person is saying: that he or she is in an emotional state in which connection with other persons seems to be lacking or absent. We may be correct anyway; after all, the synonyms of being lonely include being alone, lonesome, without company, and solitary. In common expression, people may not distinguish being alone from being lonely; they simply use either of the expressions to describe their experience of loneliness or aloneness. But a closer examination of the nature of their experiences reveals that there is a basic difference between being alone and being lonely. This is what we shall try to explore in this chapter. Then, we shall focus on the experience of loneliness and the two major forms it takes.

## To be Alone is not to be Lonely

Dictionaries describe the experience of being alone as "being apart from others; solitary; being without anyone or anything else; considered separately from all others of the same class; being without equal; unique". From this description we can notice two senses in which we can apply "being alone" to our experiences. First, "being alone" describes the uniqueness of each person. This fundamental uniqueness, the "I-ness" that underlies and qualifies the existence of every human being, is largely beyond the grasp of other persons. "It is a solemn truth", writes William Alger "that, in spite of his manifold intercourses, and after all his gossip is done, every man, in what is most himself, and in what is deepest in his spiritual relationships, lives alone"[1]. Or as Raymond Chapman analogously expresses: "The solitary pine on a distant ridge may inspire romantic feelings, but they are feelings not shared by the pine"[2]. In this existential sense, being alone refers to a person's experience of being separate from others, of being different from every other person, and without equal. This is the sense in which we can say that every human being is alone in the very intimacy of his or her being; no two persons are the same, even identical twins. This is what we express when we affirm that each person is without duplicate; every human being is a world in itself.

The existential sense of being alone leads also to its social aspect, which the dictionary describes as 'being without anyone or anything else; being solitary". This description is relevant because though each person is unique and alone in the depth of his or her person, human beings are also relational, social beings. We need and seek the company of others because we affirm and consolidate our uniqueness in relationship with others. However, it may happen, and does happen, that there are times we are not just in the company of others, either as a choice we make (as when we want to be by ourselves to reflect, think, or pray and commune with God) or as circumstances permit (as when friends or family members are not around or have traveled). In such moments of aloneness, we come in touch with our existential uniqueness. Though people fill our lives and help us define ourselves, situations exist when we are made to come to terms, either by circumstances or by choice with the uniqueness of our persons.

From the discussion so far, it should be clear that being alone does not necessarily imply being unhappy; it is not a negative experience. It is because of this that we sometimes choose to be alone and make positive use of it. As a matter of fact, life also demands we take some time to be alone and reflect about our life, what goes well and what does not go well, and about where our life may be going. It is in those moments that we come face to face with the particularity of our existence, the personal nature of our destiny, and the uniqueness of the path we tread through life. Such are the moments we challenge ourselves with regard to the ultimate meaning of our lives. A second point we notice in being alone is that, even though one may be alone either by choice or by circumstance, the individual still feels connected to persons, whether they are near or far, and to God. Friends can be thousands of miles away from each other, but they are connected to each other in their hearts. There are times also when we may be alone but we feel deeply connected to God. So, physical aloneness does not necessarily imply emotional aloneness which would aptly describe the inner state that is called loneliness.

To be lonely is generally a painful emotional experience. A lonely person is one who is "destitute of sympathetic or friendly companionship or relationships; remote from places of human habitation; isolated, lonesome, lacking companionship, forlorn, forsaken". Such a person *feels* isolated, dejected, abandoned, empty, disconnected or alienated from people; he or she is cut-off from relationships. Whether alone or in the midst of persons a lonely person feels isolated or excluded from other persons. It is an experience that can destabilize one's entire life, and can lead to series of psychological and physical illness.

As you must have noticed, the context of loneliness is relationship. It should not be difficult to understand that we desire to love and to be loved. It is in receiving and giving love that we blossom with life, we know ourselves as having value, and

4

are energized to develop ourselves and help in creating a more conducive human community. It is in the network of our relationships that we affirm both our independence from (aloneness) and our dependence on others. It is this fulfilling human relationship which *is perceived* to be absent from the life of a lonely person. That the absence of fulfilling relationship "is perceived" by the person is meant to emphasize that loneliness is largely a state of the mind formed from a combination of circumstances, external and internal.

A major difference exists therefore between being alone and being lonely, and J.O. Sanders captures this difference clearly: "being alone involves physical separation, but being lonely includes both spiritual and psychological isolation. [Loneliness] produces ... the feeling of being cut off from others whom we should like to have as friends"[3].

## Two Major Forms of Loneliness

There is not an agreed classification of loneliness. Authors tend to classify the experience of loneliness according to the aspect of it they want to explore. R.S. Weiss distinguishes two kinds of loneliness: emotional loneliness and social loneliness. Emotional loneliness occurs in the loss of a significant person such as a spouse or a close friend; social loneliness is what people experience when an engaging social network of relationships is lacking[4]. In other words, emotional loneliness indicates absence of intimate relationships while social loneliness means that one is not having the kind of interpersonal interaction one desires. For Dan Kiley, loneliness is experienced differently by "uncoupled" persons (that is, people who are not married or living together) and "coupled" persons (that is, persons who are married or living together). The difference in the two expresses two forms of loneliness. He devotes his book, *Living Together, Feeling Alone*, to exposing LTL – Living Together Loneliness, that is, coupled loneliness. Writing from a more philosophical perspective, Clark Moustakas differentiates between existential loneliness in which a person feels alone in life and in one's various experiences, and loneliness anxiety, which is basically a psychological problem characterized by alienation from self and from life and nature[5]. He further divides existential loneliness into the loneliness of solitude which is "a peaceful state of being alone with the ultimate mystery of life – people, nature, the universe – the harmony and wholeness of existence"; and the loneliness of a broken life, which is experienced when life becomes "shattered by betrayal, deceit, rejection, gross misunderstanding, pain, separation, illness, death, tragedy, and crisis that severely alter not only one's sense of self, but the world in which one lives, one's relationships, and work projects"[6].

These classifications are helpful in so far as they lead us to a deeper understanding of the dimensions of the experience. The emphasis of each author seems to have determined the nature of his or her classification. But, from the classifications of various authors I feel that two broad forms of loneliness could be delineated. The first I call existential loneliness in agreement with Moustakas' understanding of the concept. However, I would limit this form of loneliness to the existential quest of each human being for the meaning of life, and the relationship we have with life as a whole and with God. The path that leads to that meaning is a lonely one, lived and experienced by every individual in a way not comparable to the path of anyone else. His concept of the loneliness of a broken life is part of the existential loneliness only in so far as the experiences of life's brokenness remain intimate to persons so that they are difficult to be shared fully by another person. The second could be called social loneliness because it expresses the loneliness we feel in the context of our relationship with other human persons: friends, colleagues, spouses, family members, significant persons in our lives, and so on. Though the degree of intimacy in these relationships differs from one group to the other, they all derive from our nature as social beings. Because of this, I am inclined to see Weiss' distinction between emotional and social loneliness in the present context as unnecessary. I will now go ahead to examine these two major forms of loneliness in detail.

## *Existential Loneliness*

Existential loneliness derives from what could be described as "the utter subjectivity of human existence[7]". This philosophical expression simply means that our experiences are subjective irrespective of the objective nature of the circumstances that might have triggered them off. In other words, no matter how connected you are, no matter how close you are with other persons; no matter how deeply other persons share in or influence your destiny, choices, joys, sorrows, encounters, projects, these experiences bear the mark of your person as an individual. Clark Moustakas expressed this aptly when he described the lonely situation of his five-year-old daughter, Kerry, who had a congenital heart defect and had undergone a heart surgery. He tried his best to share in his daughter's pain and agony. But he realized that "no matter how fervently I lived through it with her, how much I wanted to share it with her, I knew she was alone, beyond my reach. I wanted so much for her to feel my presence, but she could not. She was beyond my call, beyond the call of anyone. It was her situation in a world entirely and solely her own"[8]. With all the love of a father, Clark wanted to share intimately with the pain of his daughter, but he could not get to the deepest subjective world of Kerry where the pain is so personal and almost impossible to share with another. At that level, we each feel lonely. Other examples abound.

Nneka is the only daughter of her parents. There are five children in the family: four boys and Nneka. Moreover, she is the last child. Their mother died when Nneka was still in elementary school. Now, the way Nneka experienced the death of their mother is different from the way her brothers experienced it. No matter how she tries to express that experience, there is something that she will never be able to express. That aspect that is impossible to express indicates the "utter subjectivity" of her existence as an individual.

Again, Victor finds it so difficult to explain to his friends why and how he fell in love with Samantha. His friends made a list of the shortcomings they discovered in her. He kept on telling them, "you do not understand". Indeed, they did not understand because his experience of the girl is unique to him. All he can do is try his best to express it, but never fully. That part he may never succeed in explaining to his friends indicates the "utter subjectivity" of his experience as a unique human being.

Take also the example of Paul and Bridget who have been married for twenty-three years without any child. They are happily married because they love each other. But this does not mean that they don't occasionally go through the pain of childlessness in a culture that has no mercy for childless couples! When other mothers show off their children or brag about the successes of their children, Bridget's heart bleeds in pain and agony. You can console her and be there for her; but you'll never be able to experience that pain the way she does; she alone knows the pain intimately more than any other person, not even her own husband.

Anthonia is a very attractive and brilliant girl. She finished her studies in the university and got her First Degree in Biochemistry. Her parents were optimistic to send her to do her Masters Program. She had once said that she would get her Masters Degree before she turned 23. Her parents were happy with her because she was a young, focused and promising woman. However, during her

National Youth Service, she met Adamu, a young man from Sokoto, who had a degree in Civil Engineering. The dream of a Masters Degree and further studies vanished from the consciousness of Anthonia. All she wanted was to get married to this young man and become a mother. Her parents and friends shuddered at this sudden turn of events. But Anthonia insisted that her life would not be meaningful outside being a mother and a wife to this person. Life has changed for Anthonia beyond the anticipations and expectations of parents and well-wishers. No one could make sense of this situation except Anthonia. No matter how her parents and good friends wished her well and planned out her life, Anthonia's life would remain hers to live. She must make sense of her own life. In that moment of intense attention to her life, Anthonia realized how deeply she was alone, and how she had to face up to what she considered the direction her life should take.

The main point in these examples is that these subjective experiences can never be replicated exactly by another person. The joy of having a baby, falling in love, getting your degree, having your own home, surviving an accident or sickness, getting married, may be expressed, but the experience remains largely personal. The pain of losing your loved one, being childless, unmarried or unwanted, poor, or being a failure, remains unique to the individual. Other persons can make an effort to understand and empathize, but they can never fully relate to the experience.

In all these experiences, we accept the particularity of our lives and destinies. At the same time, we desire to connect with others: we seek out persons we love and struggle to bond with them, share our stories and experiences with them, and forge great relationship with them. Thus, between this "utter subjectivity of human existence" and our desire to connect with others, there is a tension, "the tension of human co-existence"[9]. We feel that we must make sense of our lives as individuals. But we need others in order to carry out this existential project well and fully. This tension challenges our psychological and spiritual maturity; it is at the heart of many pathologies! In handling this tension, some people tend to deny or run away from the loneliness that comes from their subjective experiences by forming more or less unhealthy relationships with other persons. Such relationships are often characterized by fusion rather than interdependence. These are persons who expect others, be they friends or life partners, to take away the existential loneliness that marks their uniqueness as individuals. At the other extreme are those who feel so oppressed and weighed down by their loneliness that they lose trust or hope in close relationships. These persons have disengaged from life and from persons, and have exaggerated the loneliness of human existence. In between these two extremes are other persons who are inclined more or less towards close relationship with others or away from it.

It does not end here. As we struggle to live as individuals and in relationship with others, we go through many experiences that provoke questions and thoughts that are of ultimate concern - experiences like unrealized dreams, failed projects, bad decisions, relationships that have soured, growing old, sickness, betrayal, deceit, loss of a loved one or job, failure, economic upheaval, and the unrestrained progression of life towards death. These experiences make us question the meaning of our lives. Though we may have friends, companions, family members who stand by us during these experiences, the responsibility to make sense of them remains our own. In all the events and changes that happen in one's life, one must find meaning to go on living, otherwise one falls into despair and hopelessness. No one can do it for the other. Nkechi is now approaching forty years, and she has not got married. People have come up with various explanations about why she is not married. Some tell her that she has been bewitched by her enemies; others say her destiny has been locked up by mermaid spirits. Some others believe that some ancestral spirits are at work in her family. Whether she follows these explanations or runs away from the existential situation is up to her. If she must go on living, she must find meaning in that condition irrespective of the demands that the culture makes on her. Jonathan was once a successful business man. After some years of economic glory, his business turned upside down. He could not bear the pain of these changes. Many of his friends tried to console him, and others gave him advice. Some told him that a jealous person had charmed away all his money; his closest friend asked him to think clearly if there was no one who had it in for him. If he has to go on living, he must make sense of the situation; otherwise, he could pursue seen and unseen enemies all the remaining days of his life. Or, consider a couple that married for just two years. After the woman had given birth to their first child, she was diagnosed with cancer. She died in their third year of marriage. The husband must go on living, and if he must, he needs to find meaning and motivation for it.

These experiences make urgent the question of the meaning of our lives; they make us ask personal questions: where am I going really? Where is my life heading? Does life have meaning at all? Is life simply eating, making money, marrying and having children, being popular, or is there something more? Must everything go well with me as I want it? Is misfortune evil at all? Or, does it have meaning in the grand scale of life? We may try to avoid paying attention to these questions by invoking excuses or playing blame games; but we may not succeed all the time. Life has a way of forcing them on us, sometimes when we least expect it. To each of these questions we must render a personal response; no one takes the place of the other just as no one actually dies another person's death.

As we go through these life events and changes and reflect on the meaning of our lives, we realize that we are deeply lonely at the core of our being. This existential loneliness is actually what makes us aware of the impermanence of things, including human life itself. Existential loneliness is therefore a double-edged sword: it can lead to despair, which is basically a loss of meaning and motivation; but it can also be the window through which we catch a glimpse of the spiritual dimension of human life before which the glory of everything in this world vanishes and loses its enslaving fascination. In this latter sense, existential loneliness could be a painful experience of renewal and redemption in which the individual acknowledges his or her contingency and seeks a true and liberating relationship with the transcendent God who makes all things new and meaningful. Many people have discovered in their lives that it is in this leap of faith in God that the agony of existential loneliness is overcome. For such people, their experience of loneliness has become a strong motivation to seek union with God in whom they place their faith. The essence of this faith is obedience, in which the human being accepts his finitude and the fact that his life has ultimate meaning in his relationship with God[10]. This new awareness reconnects the individual to the root of his being, God, in a very conscious and radical manner. Such an experience is actually the birth of conscious religious life that is profound and liberating. Before then, faith or religion might have remained mostly functional, an unconscious psychological placation of the Divine for the disquiet of the mind and a struggle to 'use' the transcendent God to modify one's existential condition[11].

Existential loneliness is, therefore, part of our human condition. It is inevitable. It is the means through which we get a fuller sense of what it means to be a human being. At the same time, it could become the ultimate avenue through which we are alienated from the ground of our being, and so surrender to despair and self-annihilation[12].

## *Social Loneliness*

Social loneliness is what we are more accustomed to. It is what we experience when we feel isolated, excluded, rejected, without connection, abandoned or neglected. It is in this sense that Rook defines loneliness as "an enduring condition of an emotional state that arises when a person feels estranged from, is misunderstood or rejected by, and/or lacks appropriate social partners for a desired activity, particularly activities that provide a sense of social integration and opportunities for emotional intimacy"[13]. The key experience in social loneliness is lack or absence of emotional intimacy. In other words, there could be people around with whom one relates, but the individual feels little or no emotional connection or intimacy.

This is not difficult to understand. You may have experienced that sometimes when you are in certain groups - for example study group, prayer group, or just a group with common interests. After some time, you will start to notice whether you are emotionally connected to the group or not. This happens automatically because we seek to feel connected with others. For this reason, we are very sensitive to any act, real or perceived, of exclusion. You may begin to feel that some persons in the group are more bonded than others. At that time, you may begin to complain that the members don't talk to you as they talk to each other; sometimes, they do not ask your opinion in certain matters; no one seems to notice if you are there or not. Whether these external factors are true or not, you *feel* that you are left out of the group. You may be attending all their meetings, participating in all the discussions and outings, but you still feel emotionally distant from that group. You are there but not completely because your heart is not so involved. You feel you are emotionally alienated. You are in the midst of this group but no one knows you are there; it would seem you have no name, no face. This is social loneliness.

Children and adults feel lonely in this way. Parents may be preoccupied with providing material things for their children but without giving personal attention to them. They have no time to admire their children, compliment them, do certain things together with them, and show some interest in them. They feel satisfied that their children are well-fed and well-provided for. Others are too busy with making more money that they have little or no time to chat with their children. It is good to work hard to feed children and pay their school fees. But presence is also very important. Amandi had everything he needed as a child of educated parents who had good jobs. He lacked nothing except the warmth of his parents. The Dad was always busy with working for his promotion in the university, and the Mom was always attending one conference or another. Amandi grew up practically with their maid, Nkiru. He became more attached to Nkiru than to his parents. This became obvious when he got into the university. He came home mostly to collect what he needed but stayed more in the house of his friends. It was his Mom who began to observe the uneasiness of Amandi each time he came home. In the course of talking with Amandi, it dawned on the parents that parenting is more than giving material things to the child; presence is fundamental.

At other times, parents emotionally isolate their children without knowing it; and this can be devastating to the child. Nnenne is the first child of her parents. At the age of 16 she became pregnant with her first child, and stopped going to school. After two years of being at home, she resumed school. In her 20th year, Nnenne was pregnant the second time. This brought so much shame to her parents and brothers and sisters. Nnenne seemed not to care about the situation. On listening to Nnenne's story, it could be observed that she was deeply lonely; she felt rejected by both her father and mother. Her father was disappointed that his first child was a girl, and her mother shared in the disappointment. So, they treated Nnenne as if her birth was a mistake to be regretted. Nnenne's immediate junior was a boy. All attention was given to him, and it was like Nnenne did not exist. She hardly received compliments from her parents; everything she did was bad. As her younger brother grew up, the rivalry between the two became an occasion for her parents to punish her for coming into the world. From her childhood, Nnenne felt she was not loved; she was not accepted; she was an accident, and, psychologically, she lived as an emotionally isolated child. Nnenne's 'wild' lifestyle became a way of dealing with her loneliness.

A child also could feel socially lonely in school. He or she may be taunted by peers or humiliated by teachers and/or left out in an event that involved other children. In these situations, children feel abandoned, or rejected; they feel lonely. Those children feel unwanted and unrecognized; no one wants them! It can be an awful feeling for a child.

There are various situations where adults too feel lonely. For instance, one may feel isolated from colleagues at work or in school when one feels not up to the standard; a man also may feel socially lonely because he does not have a male child and this makes him feel inadequate among his peers; a woman may also feel socially isolated because her friends have become mothers in their own homes and she is still in her father's house; another may feel estranged in a group because he or she did not have a degree. A beloved may become suddenly lonely and her lover appears very strange. This we shall explore more deeply in the life of married people.

As can be seen, social loneliness is always connected to our social relationships, intimate or less intimate. The key idea is that the socially lonely person *feels* emotionally distanced from the relevant relationship. This can take place in family, among friends, in the workplace, among colleagues, and in any other social network in which one is involved. These social networks present different degrees of intimacy. In spite of these relationships and the relational satisfaction they provide us, we still yearn for some person or persons before whom we could be completely ourselves, unguarded and free to share the depth of who we are. Fundamentally, therefore, the essence of social loneliness is that difficulty in having someone with whom to share one's soul.

Certain life events necessarily bring about social loneliness such as bereavement, separation, breakup of relationships, abandonment, betrayal, divorce, and so on. In these moments, the emotional bond from which an individual has lived is severed. Different support groups enable us go through these painful emotional moments. But it is these life events that usually force us to think about the meaning of life, our own lives in a serious manner. Here, we find the link between social and existential loneliness: from our experience of social loneliness we are led by the situations of life to experience the loneliness of our individual existence, that "utter subjectivity of human existence" we talked about in the preceding section. In each situation, two ways are open to us: the way of redemption through reorganization of previous systems of meaning and the way of despair in which life becomes a burden of meaninglessness that leads to a hopeless death of the individual. Loneliness, therefore, has serious effects on the individual, physical and psychological.

# Loneliness: Physical and Psychological Effects

In general, loneliness can have serious effects on our physical and mental health. However, its psychological effect on people is more recognized and documented than its physical impact. In fact, James J. Lynch, a medical scientist, suspects a kind of schizophrenia between the attitude of medical scientists and common sense when it comes to the physical consequences of loneliness. He reasons that human beings know from a very long time ago that "their fellow men die of broken hearts"[14], and yet medical science is slow in acknowledging this as a relevant aspect of diagnosis. For him, the best way to approach the relationship of loneliness to the physical health of human beings is to examine the role human contact plays in the health of our hearts.

The health of the human heart, he argues, "depends not only on such factors as genetics, diet, and exercise, but also to a large extent on the social and emotional health of the individual"[15]. Human touch, the comforting words of friends and family members, the presence of loved ones, are found to have positive impact on the health of the human heart. In other words, human companionship effects some positive changes on our body chemistry[16]. This implies that lack of human contact, absence of human companionship, can have debilitating effects on people. Just in the same manner, "those individuals who lack the comfort of another human being may very well lack one of nature's most powerful antidotes to stress"[17]. This means that lonely individuals "are particularly vulnerable to stress and anxiety"[18]. It does not matter whether they are married or single.

Psychologically, loneliness has been generally associated with low self-esteem, depression, anxiety, vulnerability to stress, interpersonal hostility, agitation, and feeling of emptiness. In a study on loneliness and the effects it has on life-changes on 633 subjects, 295 men and 338 women, Ami Rokach found out that emotional distress stood out as "the most salient feature of the experience of loneliness"[19]. Emotional distress would include two groups of emotional states: first, agony and turmoil, which express the "intense feelings of anguish", and secondly, emptiness and hopelessness, which "describe the sense of void and lack of control over one's destiny that pervades the lonely individual's life"[20]. These are symptoms of depression, which, itself, has been consistently found to correlate positively with the feelings of loneliness[21]. On July 6, 2004, a story was carried in the England's *Daily Mail*, about an 86 year old woman, Margaret O'Riordan, who slumped into depression and died in a nursing home after she was told she could not keep the door to her bedroom open. Before her death, she had complained to her nephew: "What's the point living if I can't speak to people? I can't even say hello to my friends". There are also some women in our African-Igbo culture who die from depression as a result of loneliness they feel for being unmarried and being made fun of by other people, especially the wives of their brothers. The same is true of certain childless couples who feel they are different from other married men and women, and therefore, lonely.

Loneliness resulting from rejection, abandonment, betrayal, social exclusion, has also been found to be a factor in some addictive behaviours such as compulsive sexual acting out, excessive drinking and eating, involvement in drugs, and others. These addictive behaviours become ways some lonely persons seek to drown their loneliness and hold thinly to life. In the November 13, 1996 edition of *Daily Mail*, it was reported that Gina Malik, the 41 years old wife of the Film Star, Art Malik, started using cannabis, in order to lift herself out of the depression she got into as a result of the loneliness she felt due to her husband's long absences while filming. Nicky Cruz, a Puerto Rican boy wrote the story of his lonely life in his classic book, *Lonely, But never Alone*. He experienced series of rejection and abandonment from his parents. At one time, his mother called him devil in front of other women and shouted at him to "Get away, devil! Get out of here. Do you hear? GET OUT!"[22] Nicky felt neither his Dad nor his Mom wanted him; he was deeply lonely. So, he ran away from home and country and migrated to the United States where he engaged in all sorts of life of gangsterism in upstate New York. When he became a changed person through his experience of the unconditional love of God in Jesus Christ, he came to write from his experience: "Loneliness has many names – delinquency, alcoholism, psychiatric problems, physical illness, drug addition, nervous breakdown, suicide, divorce"[23].

It is, therefore, obvious that loneliness can have a series of negative impacts on our physical and mental health. This is true because we are social beings, made for relationship and companionship. No man or woman is an island. But this companionship is more than just being together; it entails the valuing of each other as persons of dignity, persons of worth. Without this reflection of personal worth in relationship, persons can be together and still remain lonely; a situation we will investigate in detail in the remaining chapters of this book.

## The Pain of being Married and Lonely

It was Ami Rokach who wrote that "being lonely is painful, but being married and lonely can be excruciating"[24]. Lonely married people would agree with this observation. The excruciating pain of being married and lonely is the state of unhappiness in which lonely married people usually find themselves, sometimes with a floating feeling of helplessness. No human being is happy all the time; there are happy and unhappy times. But in the case of many lonely married men and women, the emotional state of unhappiness is more or less prolonged, taking a great toll on their time, thinking, and energy. Lonely husbands and wives feel empty and sad within themselves, and since marriage is expected to be a permanent union between a man and a woman, the feeling of helplessness adds weight to the emotional condition that already drains the emotional life of lonely married men and women. In the industrialized parts of the world, divorce has become the easiest way of escaping from this trap of unhappiness. But divorce itself does not resolve most of the problems associated with marital loneliness; it rather creates more problems for the divorcees and their children. At the same time, staying together in marriage does not mean that the couples are the happiest; it could be a very destructive kind of living together. In both situations, loneliness is felt strongly and has devastating effects on the couples. My interest is focused on couples living together, and how they would know, understand, and deal with their loneliness especially when it sets in. But most importantly, my objective is to help prevent it.

Marital loneliness has emotional, moral, aesthetic, and spiritual effects on couples and their family. Emotionally, the lonely husband or wife tends to be more aggressive than normal, irritated and prone to lashing out at the least provocation. Lonely wives tend to be emotionally volatile; often their emotions get out of hand. In some cases, however, the emotions are turned inward and they become somehow withdrawn, timid, and sluggish in their speech, posture or appearance. The more aggressive women tend to be restless and irritable and the less aggressive ones appear sluggish and depressive. Men tend to mask their loneliness through drinking, excessive engagement in work, travels, and outdoor activities. At home, they can be aggressive towards their wives and children. Most importantly, lonely husbands and wives can be indifferent to the emotional needs of their spouses and children because they have become so self-centered.

The feeling of loneliness in marriage could change the moral values of the couples, especially the values of love and commitment. Some lonely husbands and wives tend to seek emotional and sexual fulfillment outside their marital home. In this way, some have become emotionally detached from their spouses and unfaithful to their marital commitment. Both emotional detachment and infidelity are serious matters that affect the moral status of a marital relationship. There are certain websites that boldly target lonely married men and women who discretely look out for extra-marital affairs and other relationships. The managers of these websites make fortune out of the lonely condition of married men and women to the point of encouraging and sanctioning marital infidelity. Dennis and Barbara Rainey describe this kind of emotional flirtation as "emotional adultery" which serves as a kind of prelude to physical adultery. Emotional adultery is "unfaithfulness of the heart"[25]. When the heart of a spouse goes after another person outside the marital commitment too far as to take on an emotionally significant place more than one's spouse, then emotional adultery is at work, even when there is no sexual infidelity. It often starts with sharing one's family woes and troubles and inner life with the "lover" outside the marital home. This is different from the trust existing in a therapeutic relationship or in spiritual direction.

Aesthetically also, marital loneliness has serious effects on the family. Some lonely wives lose interest in their home and surroundings, and even in themselves. When this is the case, they tend to lack the energy to keep the house clean and in order. The scattered condition of their homes reflects the restlessness in their hearts. Sometimes, also they give up keeping themselves clean and dressing up well. It is like they have surrendered themselves to loneliness and since they can do nothing about it, they might as well go on with their lives as days come and go. On the other hand, some become obsessed with keeping everything in order as an unconscious way of feeling in control of the situation that seems to be falling apart. Some lonely husbands are also the same way. They tend to lose a sense of dignity and respect for themselves such that it does not matter to them if their home is in order or not. A good number of lonely husbands live in denial of their emotional condition and present the macho countenance that everything is under control.

Since there is emotional distance between the couples, their spiritual life is also affected. They may individually be living intense religious devotions and prayers, but these do not build their home. The union of hearts experienced by married persons has powerful spiritual implications. First, the experience of dialogue of hearts created by a genuine marital relationship liberates the spouses from self-centeredness that impedes their mutual self-gift to each other. This freedom opens up for them the mystery of their relationship as an active participation in the unity of all human beings, of cosmos, and of the unity of everything and every person in the transcendent God. Secondly, through the same dialogue of hearts, the pains and conflicts of relationships are also worked through, so that such moments become redemptive for the spouses, making them realize daily their own need of redemption. This realization broadens their understanding of how all human beings and all creation cry out for redemption also. Marital loneliness stifles the dialogue of hearts and impedes the couple's efforts at growing in interior freedom. To a reasonable degree, a lonely married person tends to be self-preoccupied with his or her lonely condition. It is a situation that can dull the mind and dim the light of the spirit. It affects the spouses and their home.

## Summary

My effort in this chapter has been to lay the foundation for the other chapters. I have been able to show the difference between being alone and being lonely. Being alone is generally a positive experience, and often chosen by the individual or thrust upon him or her by circumstances. On the contrary, being lonely is generally a painful experience which could lead one to a deeper understanding of life and reorganization of personal meaning or it could lead to a shrinking of one's life and utter despair. In the following chapter, I shall examine the phenomenon of marital loneliness, its nature and the various manifestations of it..

# II

## ANATOMY OF MARITAL LONELINESS

*If there's one thing worse than a miserable, lonely single, it's a miserable, lonely married person.*
　　　　　　　 – Dennis & Barbara Rainey

Marital loneliness is basically a problem of intimacy. It is often the case that married people who are lonely do not know what is happening to them, or when the internal desolation started. Unaware of what is happening to them, they tend to behave in an erratic and self-defeating manner. They feel that something is not going well in their lives and in their marriage, but they seem unable to figure out what it is. The tragic marriage of Prince Charles and Diana, the Princess of Wales, presents a modern classic story of marital loneliness. We shall narrate the story later in this chapter. In a religiously intense culture like the African-Igbo, a noticeable tendency of lonely married persons is to escape into some religious groups and religious practices. Gradually, they acquire the habit of giving more time to the activities in the Church than to their families. At least, they are not flirts, and most people would admire their dedication to religion. Yet, they do not miss their marital home when they are away, except for their children; they are fathers and mothers, but their spousal relationship is hunting them. Some men also learn to stay away late from their homes. These escapist attitudes could go on for months and years and the couple would not listen to their hearts or admit that something is not going well with them. Some settle down to the situation and derive some passing peace from their children; others have learned to live with the condition and, from time to time, they quarrel and ease off their pains and frustrations.

When married people feel lonely, they should know that something is not going well with their relationship. It could be that there wasn't intimacy between the couples or that the existing intimacy is being lost. In this chapter, I shall try to do some kind of diagnosis of the situation. I shall present some of the signs and symptoms of this problem which is often masked in many ways. All the symptoms point to the nature of the spousal relationship. The objective is to help couples learn to listen to themselves and identify when this problem is setting in and start early on to face it.

# Signs and Symptoms of Marital Loneliness

*Emotional Vacancy: Living together but Lonely*

The principal sign that the relationship between couples is losing its importance in their lives is the experience of emotional vacancy, where the couples live together but do not feel much emotional attachment to each other. It is the situation in which a spouse feels lonely in the arms of the other spouse. This experience is not the same thing with the decline of the romantic glow that is generally expected in romantic relationships. Most people in mature and stable relationships realize that their love relationship will not always be in the upbeat of romantic ecstasy. In those periods of low emotions, they are still emotionally present to each other in their mutual discovery of the enduring goodness of each other. To expect a relationship to remain permanently at the level of romantic dramatization is to believe in a myth which will be sooner or later shattered by experience. People with such expectation are generally immature, and will find it difficult to engage themselves in any meaningful and lasting relationship whether they are married or not.

Emotional vacancy expresses that internal state one finds oneself in when one no longer feels emotionally related to one's wife or husband. It could happen between the two of them, that is, it could be mutual or just to one. When this is the case, one begins to experience one's spouse as a kind of stranger in the house. His or her actions in this period time become annoying to one. One feels that there is some distance, a kind of wall that has gone up without one knowing when it started and who erected it. Through all the cultural and legal processes, one has become officially husband and wife. By the grace of God, one has also become a parent, doing everything possible to take care of the children. One feels culturally secure as a married person, and as a mother or a father. Despite all this, however, one still feels something is missing between oneself and one's spouse; that there is some kind of coldness in the relationship. One feels isolated and left out of his or her heart. Or, one feels he or she is not truly and firmly planted in the spouse's heart. In other words, one does not experience the spouse as the object of one's emotions of love and relationship. One shares the same bed, makes love, discusses the children's future and finances, eats together and does one's duties as husband and wife. Most of the time, however, one does these things because one should do them. That is good because love is also a duty. But, the major issue is that one feels that one doesn't really share one's life with the spouse: he or she is emotionally distant from one just as one is from him or her. One doesn't feel any spontaneity to share one's worries, joy, happiness, with him or her unless they are matters that concern the children and how to keep them well. Even if one wants to share one's experiences with one's spouse, one is afraid one may not be listened to or be understood. From all indications you really live together, "but you don't share life with one another"[1]. When you go through these internal experiences, you may be experiencing emotional vacancy towards your husband or wife. It is a situation best described as physical proximity without emotional presence. This implies that the mere living together of married persons does not mean that their hearts, minds, and emotions are given or made available to each other. This should be the ideal situation, but the real experiences of many married people do not reflect that ideal, just like many things in human life. In her study on loneliness, Ami Rokach found out that the first factor that emerged among the married members of the group she studied was interpersonal isolation. According to her, this factor includes experiences of loss of intimacy, feelings of abandonment and pain[2].

Three years after they got married, Chinenye started experiencing an unusual feeling towards her husband Linus. She described her situation as "lack of feeling". In actual fact, she has feelings towards Linus, but they are mostly feelings of agitation, anger and even contempt. Every small thing that her husband does annoys her: his manner of dressing, walking, eating, and talking; everything he does is a problem. She complains that her husband does not dress well, that he smells, that he is shy and weak and not like his friend Celestine who is hardworking; that he eats too much and does not think about tomorrow; that he does not have social value; that he does not have taste; that he is timid; that he does not wash his mouth well, and so on; a litany of his sins and incompetence! As Chinenye continued pouring out these 'sins' of her husband,

Linus, she came to the point that she could no longer hold her emotions, and so, she burst into tears and cried out: "I'm tired of this marriage; tired of him; tired of everything and everybody". She has been talking to her husband like this close to ten months, and her Linus had even withdrawn more and more to himself and talked less. He would not have time to talk with his wife; he simply commands and makes sure that his commands are obeyed with precision. With time, Linus, whom Chinenye described as soft-spoken and caring before they got married, had become a terror to be feared. No matter how tensed the situation may be, Linus makes sure that any day he wants to have sex from her, Chinenye should not dare refuse, for, according to him, "I paid for it!" She had tried once, and he nearly broke her jaw. Her friends had warned her never to try that again for no one would understand if she were to make a case of it. So, as she said, she would just lie down for him and he would "do his thing and leave, and I will continue with my life. As for me, I have no sexual interest in him after seven months of our marriage".

This situation became so nasty and dangerous for the couple and for their children before they could create the occasion to look at what was happening to them. Without knowing when and how, Linus and Chinenye had gradually become isolated from each other and suffered terrible pain from that. They constantly worked themselves up and lived in a kind of hell. But the major reason was that they had become emotionally distant from each other and their physical proximity became somehow oppressing to them. Those intimate experiences that used to be gestures of their oneness like eating together, making love, mutual enjoyment of their children, attending social events together, gradually became burdensome and avoided if possible. Yet, they lived together.

Emotional vacancy does not necessarily imply lack of feeling; it is more an internal state in which a spouse feels the other spouse is a kind of stranger; a nuisance that could generate feelings of anger and agitation. The anger could be turned towards the other spouse as in the case of Chinenye and Linus, or it could be turned inwards to the self. In both cases, the couple suffers the pain of isolation, a significant symptom of loneliness.

## *Communication is more Technical than Personal*

When emotional vacancy sets in, it shows itself in the communication between the spouses. First of all, the couples lose interest and joy in talking to each other. The desire to tell stories and share one's experiences also lessens or even dries up. Secondly, and most importantly, when they have to communicate, it turns out to be more technical than personal.

Communication between people in a love relationship is personal when they are able to say things the way they personally feel about them. It is technical if they merely stay at the level of observation of what is good and not-so-good but without reference to the way it touches them. The basic difference between technical and personal

34

communication is that "technical communication doesn't have a sense of self. This is the hallmark of alienation"[3]. A good example of a technical communication is what a man said to his wife four days after he had eaten a delicious *Egusi* soup the wife had made: "I think that soup you made few days ago was good". He was finding a way of asking her to make the same soup again for his friends who were coming for some celebration at their house. Then he added: "I think it would be good for our friends". He is making a general observation concerning the soup and was drawing a logical suggestion from that observation: since the soup is a good one, it is good enough to be served to his friends. That is all. Consider a husband in the same situation saying to his wife: "I loved the *Egusi* soup you made few days ago; could you make it for our friends". You notice immediately the sense of self contained in the second case: this husband is giving his own personal experience of his wife's cooking and is making a personal request. Such self-referential communication is a gesture of love, and has the capacity to release energy in the spousal relationship. When communication between spouses is becoming increasingly technical, it could be expressing some emotional distance between them.

Take another classic example. Ngozi was away in Ghana on some in-service training organized by the company she was working for. Her husband, Martin, is a bank manager. They have been married for about eight years. From the third year of their marriage, Ngozi had started feeling unease about

35

their marriage. They had had some disagreements and quarrels, but not too often. Somehow, she sensed that Martin had become too cold towards her, but she could not identify what it was. Her feeling would become stronger and more intense when she went to Ghana for the training. During that period, she e-mailed her husband telling him how things were going with her, and asked him about the children and the maid looking after their children. She told him how she was missing him, and how she longed to come home as soon as the training was over. In addition, she also told him that such a temporary separation had made her realize how important he and the family were to her. She concluded the mail by reaffirming her love for him this way: "you are my darling husband, and I will love you forever". Her husband replied the e-mail after five days (the training lasted for two weeks) and simply told her that everything was going well. Then he went ahead to tell her about the uneasiness in the State and the political fallouts in their town. At the end he wished her well and concluded: "You are cherished; you are missed!" It was like all the personal experiences the wife told him were not heard or even experienced. Ngozi became terrified and somehow confirmed in her feeling that some unknown but felt wall had come between her and Martin.

As you must have observed, Martin's communication to Ngozi is very technical, devoid of reference to self. Ngozi's communication is personal and you will expect her to feel estranged emotionally from Martin. Ngozi contained her anger towards what she perceived as Martin's insensitivity, until she came home. When she came back, the situation had become worse. She felt a certain kind of emotional doom about to fall on her and her family. So many thoughts competed in her mind: maybe Martin has another woman in his life; maybe she is not doing her duty as a wife; maybe she is no longer beautiful; maybe someone is gossiping about her and tearing her husband away from her; maybe, maybe. She could not keep her mind free of these thoughts. One day she voiced to Martin her feeling that something was happening between them. She gave him instances, including his insensitive e-mail. Martin became angry and accused her of trying to monitor him. There was no discussion that evening but shouts and throwing of aggressive words here and there. The only good thing was that it happened in their bedroom. From then on, Ngozi became afraid to share her experiences with Martin except things that concerned their children. They had drifted farther and farther away from each other. Ngozi had sensed the emotional vacancy of her husband towards her but it was Martin's technical communication that confirmed her experience of marital loneliness. She could not understand the situation; she had hoped that marrying an educated man would have made it easier for them to communicate. She became disillusioned, isolated, abandoned, and in pain.

Communication is the life-wire of any relationship. Through it spouses understand each other better, become more aware of themselves, and deepen their relationship. Because of its importance in any relationship, it serves as a kind of thermometer with which the emotional temperature of a relationship is measured. In the technical message of Martin, Ngozi had read that the emotional bond between them had become too low. Her effort to dialogue with her husband at a personal level did not work; it sent the message clearly to her that something was seriously wrong. She had begun to feel alienated from Martin's heart. It did not take people time to notice that Ngozi and Martin had become two islands living parallel to each other. Their friends took sides in trying to outdo the other in gossip; and the gap in their relationship widened. As Suzzane Leonard clearly puts it: "Once there is a decline in the quality of the marital relationship, it sets off a downward cascade that is hard to reverse without active effort. Partners may remain unhappily married for a considerable period of time before starting to consider splitting up. Eventually, loneliness sets in and spouses begin to lead parallel lives. As they do, they may become susceptible to the attention of others"[4].

A subtle way technical communication happens in our African-Igbo culture is to mask the technicality with religious expressions. This method is so successful in that it is difficult to notice the absence of self-present in such expressions. For instance, Mary and Livinus have been married for ten years. Mary holds a Higher National Diploma (HND) certificate in Accounting and Livinus a Bachelor of Arts (B.A.) degree in English Language. But he turned to business after his National Youth Service. Mary also has a shop where she sells children's clothes. They both are doing well in their businesses. The couple actually met during their National Youth Service, and got married after two years. Their problem started after their first child was born. Livinus began to notice that Mary had lost interest in him; that she had become cold and unresponsive to him. He felt that she was just there as a wife but her soul and heart were absent from the home. Before their relationship took this turn, Livinus had always longed to get home after the day's business and Mary would do the same. They used to tell each other the stories of their school years, the exciting experiences they had during the National Youth Service, and she used to tease him about the way he chased her and other girls. Livinus could not understand how and why such great moments lasted only for a short while. Meanwhile, Mary had become religious. She would leave her business early to go and pray in the Church; she always has a group she prays with every day. By the time she comes back, it would be late, and their supper would be late. But she did not seem to be bothered, "after all, God should be first in everything", she says. Then, one day before they went to bed, Livinus called Mary and told her his feelings about how their marriage was going down the hill; how he was feeling that she was not wholly present in their home, and this shows in all that she does. With a very calm countenance, Mary told him that Jesus was in charge of their marriage. Livinus told her that he knew that for a long time, but that Jesus would be happy if they found out what was going wrong in their marriage, so as to live better as good and happy husband and wife, father and mother. Mary murmured that "no one should stop me from serving Jesus and Virgin Mary, Our Blessed Mother". With that statement, the case was closed. Livinus got so annoyed and started shouting at her and calling her names. He threatened to bring the matter to Mary's parents. Again, without any sign of worry, Mary said she knew that her deepened religious life would upset him knowing that he was a "worldly person". Not only did she mask her technical communication with religious expressions, she also showed contempt for him. In a religiously sensitive culture like ours, such self-righteous indignation couched in religious language can pass off as an innocent expression of deep spirituality.

This has been going on for many months and Livinus had been trying to dialogue with his wife Mary at a personal level, but he always received such a religiously loaded blanket response. That last incident was unbearable to him. Being a person who was afraid of losing his public image, he refused to talk it over with anybody except his best friend who advised him to mind his business and concentrate on their children. With that decision, Livinus and Mary, though married and living together, lived separate lives in the same home. It was not long before the effects of their loneliness became evident to two of them, and to their children.

Communication can be verbal or non-verbal. This means that we may say things in words or by our behaviours and attitudes. Mary tends to communicate her emotional disenchantment towards her husband in both a verbal and non-verbal manner. She is emotionally aggressive towards him. Her self-righteous religiosity makes her feel justified to talk to her husband the way she does. But behind these words and attitudes is a lonely Mary making unconscious efforts to deny her loneliness. Her religious cover-up did not last too long and she got into unhealthy relationships with her 'religious' friends. Then her world crumbled and her loneliness emerged in a frightening manner that could not be hidden anymore from the public. Her husband came to her rescue, and they had to seek help.

Religious expressions can mask cold communications that do not have a sense of self. It is usually subtle and successful. But, like all technical communications in relationships, they are not helpful in nurturing and building relationships. Such religiously technical expressions in marital relationship are more harmful simply because they appear harmless and innocent. We shall return to this topic in the next chapter.

## *Stalemated Communication*

This is the situation where the spouses communicate but they hardly understand or listen to each other. They do not communicate at the same level, and so their talks are prone to misunderstanding and misinterpretation. The consistency with which this happens leads to a lot of anger and disgust with and towards each other. In the end, the spouses wear each other and themselves out in trying to communicate because they have become so edgy that their talks do not get the attention they deserve. The difference between technical communication and stalemated communication is that in the former, there is absence of emotional involvement, and in the later, there is more a voicing out of one's frustration in a way that feels like hitting a wall. In stalemated communication, there is a total block in both speaking, listening and empathizing. Stalemated communication is so frustrating that oftentimes, the couples in the situation simply shout at rather than talk to each other. The other is experienced as a stranger, a wall that is hard to penetrate. Just as it can be frustrating to talk to a wall when no one is around to listen, so do a couple caught up in stalemated communication feel. But, the stalemate is merely a symptom of the loneliness the couple feels.

Henry dreads talking to his wife Philomena just as she hates discussing with him. Their conversations always end in angry walkout and denunciation of each other. As is expected, the more they fight and call each other names, the more they feel estranged from each other. They live like two islands. They struggle to talk but it always ends up in bursts of anger and crying spells. For five years they have lived in a section of the city, neighbours have become used to their fights. On one occasion, Philomena, a pharmacist, tells Henry, himself an accountant, that "this is simply silly and ridiculous. I can't go on living like this". Henry tells her to gather herself together and look for her father's house. "You are a naughty and hopeless woman", he says. Philomena looks straight into his eyes and gently says: "Each time you say something, you demonstrate that you have no brains in your head, though you are an accountant". The stage is set for another round of angry words at each other. They get exhausted before they go to sleep. Philomena notes that "I wait anxiously for daybreak because it is no use staying with a man who feels like a dead wood to you. I know what it means to live in hell. Look at me, I am aging fast despite the amount of money I make from my job. I'm sick of all this, and I don't know when it will end".

It has to be noted that couples stalemated in communication still desire to talk to each other or break through their loneliness through talking. But because they don't realize that their fighting comes from their estrangement from each other, their communication gets stalemated. This further complicates matters. The one thing good in this kind of couple is the effort, even if a misdirected one, to reach out to each other. To unblock this stalemate, the spouses need some space to do soul-searching and identify how they feel about their relationship, and what this kind of communication could mean.

### The Feeling of being Trapped and Empty

Another symptom of marital loneliness is the feeling of being trapped in the marital relationship such that one desires strongly to be relieved of this "burden" or be set free from this "prison". The feeling of being trapped expresses the experience of oneself as being unhappy and powerless in the situation: "I'm married and terribly lonely, but I cannot do anything about it. I cannot help myself!" Jane confessed and broke down in tears. She has been married for 13 years and has four children, two boys and two girls. Her husband is a handsome man with average income. Jane herself is a personal secretary to the manager of a local company. She is happy with her job. As she comes to the close of each day's job in her office, she is overcome with a feeling of fear. She is reluctant to get home because what should be a home has become for her a kind of prison without any emergency exit; she is stuck! Her happiest moments are the times she spends outside home with friends and at her place of work. She comes up with excuses to visit her parents almost every other weekend. The weekend she is to be home, instead of feeling rested, she is exhausted without doing anything outside the normal things she usually does. In the Church on Sunday, she feels great, but the moment she gets home, she becomes moody and restless. Nothing excites her. Her husband Paul has been worried about Jane's loss of enthusiasm in their marriage. He tries to come closer to her, but every step he makes feels like "another door is closed behind me with a padlock", she says. When Jane tells her story she cries profusely because she feels she has locked herself in this marriage which is "far from what I had expected". Overwhelmed with the feeling of entrapment, she loses almost the little free space she needs to listen to herself and know what is going on with her and her husband. When she listens to herself, all she hears and feels is a pounding heart that desires to be set free from a kind of relational bondage; yet, she does not know why she feels the way she does. She gets more confused because her husband is a decent man, very respectful of her, and well-respected in society. She just doesn't know how she came to where she is now. Jane is lonely and feels entrapped. After some listening sessions with Jane, she gathered the courage to admit to herself that she married Nnanna out of frustration; she wanted just to get married and escape the gossip of people against her for being an educated, beautiful but "unmarriageable girl". But now, she feels she is in a cage with Nnanna, and unable to get out. As she comes to know this, she blames herself for "such a big mistake". She is also angry towards her parents and friends who were taunting her for having "big education without a home of your own". She blames her mother for not allowing her to marry James that she had known for a long time. The blame game has not helped her; it makes her feel the pain of entrapment even stronger. Jane has fulfilled her dream to be married like any African-Igbo girl; but she experiences little or no motivation in her relationship with Nnanna; she feels helpless in the situation. "So, I'll remain like this for the rest of my life?" she asks aloud crying. Jane feels entrapped in her marriage; a feeling that gives a clue to the loneliness she is experiencing in her marriage.

If Jane feels entrapped in her marriage with Nnanna, so is Sebastian and Ezinne in their marriage. He is a successful businessman, who went into business after his first year in the university, by the prodding of his mother. Ezinne also could not finish her university degree because she got married to Sebastian in her third year in Business Administration, and got pregnant immediately. When Ezinne was in her second pregnancy, Sebastian seemed to have changed so fast: he became more aggressive, complained about almost everything at home; called Ezinne a stupid "village girl who is good only at getting pregnant". The change in behaviour was so difficult for Ezinne to understand. Gradually, Sebastian gave little attention to Ezinne, and worried only about the pregnancy, telling her to be careful that nothing happened to that child. There was a day that he got so angry towards Ezinne because their daughter resembled her. He said to her that he would not tolerate their second child, which he hoped would be a boy, to resemble her. To resemble her would be a disaster for her. Luckily, Ezinne gave birth to a healthy baby boy. Sebastian was so happy and cared for Ezinne in the first five weeks after delivery. Ezinne thanked God for the gift of the baby for she suspected that Edwin was afraid she was going to give birth to another girl. But her suspicion was to be proved wrong from the sixth week, when Sebastian returned to his dreadful aggressive outbursts. This time, he created more tension in the house. Whenever he left for business, Ezinne would hold her baby and Uchechi, their daughter, and would cry, asking God what she had done to live "in this kind of hell". One day Edwin was again raging against her, and Ezinne became angry also. She asked him what she had done to merit this kind of ill-treatment. Sebastian angrily told her that she should not ask him any question. "It was your mother and my mother that put me into this mess in order to keep their friendship", Sebastian said pointing at his wife as if she were the mess. "You know you are not qualified to be my wife, and you are asking me what you have done", he thundered.

Ezinne opened her mouth but could not say anything nor could she cry. She was overwhelmed with horror and bewilderment. She gasped for air and eventually slumped into temporary unconsciousness. Sebastian rushed her to the hospital where she was treated until she regained consciousness. He was terrified at the near death of his wife. At the same time, "I knew I wished she were dead because it was becoming a purgatory for me to go on living with her" he said. This thought terrified him also. "I would become so angry each time I looked at her and felt that I was not free from her", he confessed.

Sebastian felt entrapped and helpless in his marriage with Ezinne. The more aggressive he became towards her, the more lonely and entrapped he felt. After his wife had recovered from the shock, Sebastian thought it wise to do something positive in order to avoid killing his spouse. He decided to talk the whole situation over with Ezinne, with the help of a trusted friend of theirs who is also a psychologist. Sebastian realized that he truly loved his wife, but was rebelling against his mother whom he had always obeyed without question. The loneliness he felt in his marriage was worked through and both husband and wife regained their freedom from their mothers and became an independent and happily married couple.

The feeling of entrapment in marriage is not that easy to be identified for what it is namely, an indication of loneliness. In a sense, entrapment is in a dialectical relationship with the experience of loneliness so that we can say that a lonely married person feels entrapped and an entrapped married person feels lonely. The aggressive outbursts and constant complaints are efforts to fight against this entrapment, and the persistent feeling of helplessness despite the fights naturally lead to both mental and physical exhaustion.

Entrapment always goes with a feeling of emptiness, that feeling that one's marital life is not fulfilling. The feeling of emptiness should not surprise anyone as a significant symptom of marital loneliness. Imagine a married person coming home at the end of the day's business expecting to meet an empty house! The house is not really empty because the husband and the children, and perhaps, other relatives, are there. Yet, the anticipation of coming home to be greeted by empty house reveals the emptiness inside. Children and relatives could give a great deal of joy and fulfillment to married people. But they cannot take the place of one's spouse. When there is emotional vacancy, communication between the spouses annoys more than it refreshes. Then the couple becomes more touchy, complaining, easily provoked, and irritable. Almost anything could spark an angry response:

money, food, the arrangement in the house, children, job, hairdo, cream, shoes, laughter, and so on. This constant bickering and aggression in the house, between the spouses, wears the couple out. The fight does not resolve anything; not much positive outcome is got from it. The deterioration of the situation is frustrating, and this adds sadness to the feeling of emptiness.

## A Tragic Story of Marital Loneliness: The Prince and Princess of Wales

Diana, the Princess of Wales, was born the youngest daughter of Edward Spencer and Frances Spencer, on July 1, 1961. She married Charles, Prince of Wales on July 29, 1981. Shortly before the wedding, and through the fifteen years of their marriage, the royal couple did not find it easy. Theirs was a complicated marriage besieged by loneliness that constantly came out in persistent bickering, worry and anxiety, outbursts of anger, irrational fears and suspicion, and extra-marital affairs. The couple was separated in 1992 and their divorce became final in 1996. After their divorce, Diana lived barely one year before her fatal death in an automobile accident on August 31, 1997. On the 9th of April, 2005, Charles, Prince of Wales, married his long term love, Camilla Parker Bowles, now addressed as The Duchess of Cornwall.

The story of the marriage between Charles and Diana is the theme of many books. Sometimes the story comes close to being a kind of fairytale because of the extraordinary fascination around the personality of Diana and the pettiness that surrounded the marriage in a way that provided the press with materials about which to gossip. Whatever the stories, speculations and the facts about this enigmatic royal couple, one thing the majority of writers agree on is that the marriage was a lonely one. Authors and commentators differ on the contributions of Diana, Charles, the Queen and the whole aristocratic family and institution, to the troubles and eventual dissolution of the marriage.

Diana knew she was exquisitely beautiful, and believed she had a good chance to marry a "Mr. Royal", and precisely, it was Prince Charles she wanted[5]. When she attended a party in which Charles was present at the home of Commander Robert de Pass, she found an opportunity to sit next to her desired prince; and she did. Charles was still grieving over the death of his great-uncle, Lord Mountbatten, whom he loved so much. "Dispensing with small talk, she raised one of the most sensitive subjects imaginable, telling Charles that she had really felt for him during the televised funeral of Lord Mountbatten, and asking him how he had coped with his evident unhappiness"[6]. Such a clear demonstration of care was what someone in his situation would need. As the party wore on, Diana "told Charles how she sensed his loneliness and his need for someone to care for him. Charles found it hard to break away from this beguiling and rather beautiful young woman who seemed to understand so much about him"[7]. That incident stirred Charles' interest in Diana and his desire to see her again.

No one was in doubt as to the beauty of Diana, and her suitability as a royal bride. Charles appreciated the great warmth and enthusiasm of Diana and delighted in her. Despite these positive feelings, he confessed to one of his friends that "he was not *yet* in love with Diana, but felt that he might come to fall in love with her in time"[8].

Charles had met Camilla when he was 23 and fell in love with her. When he heard that Camilla had accepted a marriage proposal from Andrew Parker Bowles, "Charles suffered a terrible 'feeling of emptiness'"[9]. It was obvious that Charles loved Camilla with the intensity of a true first love[10], and was only *trying* to love Diana. His parents were on his back asking him to go ahead and propose to Diana or let her go if he was not sure he was going to marry her. Charles "invited Diana to Windsor Castle and asked her to marry him. He told her to take some time to think it over. She accepted immediately. Charles explained how horrendous some of the pressures would be and said it would not be an easy life. She barely listened and rushed back to Colherne Court to tell the girls"[11]. After accepting Charles' proposal, she enthusiastically told him that she loved him so much, but Charles could only say, "Whatever love means"[12]. She did not seem to care about Charles' response; she had got what she wanted: she was to be The Princess of Wales and the future Queen of England! From all indications, Diana's love for Charles was heavily mixed up with her desire to be the Princess of Wales and the future Queen. The pressure of this desire would not allow her, it seems, to listen to and process the verbal and non-verbal messages Charles was giving to her. When the press asked Diana's sister, Sarah, if she would marry the Prince, she had replied that whenever she was going to marry, it would be for love, and "that it didn't matter whether the man concerned was a prince or a dustman"[13]. She seemed wiser.

The engagement between Charles and Diana was announced on February 24, 1981. That same day, they were interviewed by BBC. The interviewers asked them if they were in love, and Diana immediately said, "Of Course", but Charles coldly added, "Whatever 'in love' means"[14], repeating exactly what he had said to her on the day he proposed to her. The emotional coldness of Charles did not seem to bother Diana at that moment. After all, the whole world was riveted on her. On the contrary, Tim Clayton and Phil Craig believe that Charles' apparent "reserve mirrored the coldly orchestrated formality of court life as it was suddenly revealed to her. She found herself under constant pressure to perform in circumstances dictated by protocol and the rigidly old-fashioned officials responsible for determining it"[15]. Whatever the coldness of the court life, it will be hard to deny that Diana's ambition to marry the Prince and become the Princess was such a heavy emotional load that did not allow her pay serious attention to Charles' love for her. Charles himself seemed unable to make a mature decision regarding Diana and Camilla, and would simply prod along. Both would realize the enormity of such emotional blindness before too long.

Before their wedding, Diana "discovered that Charles had recently sent some flowers to Camilla when she was ill with a message using what she claimed were the couple's pet names for each other: 'To Gladys from Fred'"[16]. Also within the same period, Diana had "discovered a bracelet ... with the initials 'G' and 'F' cut into it. It was intended for Camilla. Diana stormed out of the room"[17]. She pleaded with Charles not to send the present to Camilla, but Charles refused. He did send the present to Camilla in person just two days before their wedding. On that same day that Charles sent the bracelet to Camilla, Diana told her sisters that she was afraid that Charles did not love her and that she would like to withdraw from the wedding. Her sisters were said to have remarked, "Well, bad luck, Duch, your face is on the tea towels so you're too late to chicken out"[18]. And so the wedding was held and the royal couple went on their honeymoon.

Towards the end of their honeymoon, the royal couple's troubles re-emerged when the pictures of Camilla fell from Charles' diary. To make matters worse, Diana discovered that Charles wore "a pair of cuff links decorated with entwined Cs. She rightly divined that these were a gift from Camilla"[19]. Charles continued wearing that despite Diana's disapproval and anger. They quarreled and argued. This then was to become the common cycle in their marriage: Diana felt that Charles did not love her, and Charles was reluctant to address the issue; he was busy with his work as the Prince and Diana felt left alone or even lost in the vast palace with no one to talk to. She would have crying spells when she was alone, and at night she would suffer nightmarish dreams about Camilla. She was frustrated and lonely. She could not get the love she desired from Charles, and she would rage out against him. Paradoxically, "the outbursts of temper only made him more reserved when what she wanted, what she said she wanted, was his loving attention. But the more demanding she became, the more Charles viewed her with distaste"[20]. And so the gap between them widened. Diana suffered from bouts of mood swings and Charles' rage had become unpredictable and terrifying. They both felt lonely and rejected by each other but did not know how to deal with it. Under constant emotional pain of marital loneliness, they each sought emotional relief from outside their marriage and ended up in different love affairs that eventually culminated in the end of their marriage. What began as a fairytale of extraordinary beauty and royalty ended up in tragedy! In the end, Prince Charles married his second wife, who was the first true love of his life, Camilla.

The signs and symptoms of marital loneliness are evident in this story. The emotional gap between them was so clear and was the source of other difficulties that the royal couple manifested. While Diana communicated her personal feelings about their relationship, Charles stood aloof and emotionally atrophied. He was not enthusiastic about it. Their feeling of entrapment came out so vividly in their aggressive outbursts and in their search for emotional relief from outside of their marriage. The tragedy of this royal marriage could have been averted if the couples had been present to themselves enough and paid attention to their motivations. In the chapter that follows, we shall examine how and why married people can and do arrive at this stage of painful marital loneliness.

# III

## WHY AND HOW MARRIED PEOPLE ARRIVE AT LONELINESS

> *If someone is too self-focused and puts up barriers to intimacy, there can be no relationship and no intimacy. Similarly, if someone completely loses himself or herself in the union, then you have a relationship – but no intimacy.*
>
> - Paul Coleman

There is still a lot of unawareness about marital loneliness in our African-Igbo culture. This unawareness largely is due to the cultural tendency to protect family image and not expose oneself and family to public ridicule. Because of this cultural secretiveness, many lonely married couples do not know they should find out why and how their loneliness came about, and work through it. In many cases, lonely spouses who have become emotionally tuned off from each other impose upon their children to carry the burden of taking care of their loneliness. Such are the situations where parents smother their children with 'love' that ties the children perpetually to them, even when they get married. Hence we get married men and women who are unable to be attached to their spouses because of their strong attachments to their parents, especially their mothers. This chapter presents certain factors that come into play both in the foundation and in the development of marital loneliness, so that couples could use it to examine themselves as individuals and assess their marital relationship. These factors come from the shadow side of our cultural ideals and from peoples' personal desires.

## The Shadow Side of Cultural Ideals

### *The Pressure to get married and have Children*

African people believe in children, in fatherhood and motherhood. This is one of the greatest enduring values that have resisted the onslaught of the individualistic trends in the cultures of the West. All political, financial or educational achievements are literally useless without marriage and children. This great and envious value has its shadow side: it imposes so much psychological stress on young men and women to marry and have children, whether they like it or not. No man is fully a man who does not have his own wife, children and home, and no woman is fully a woman who is not a wife and a mother. For instance, among the Igbo people, "in addition to boosting one's self-esteem in the society, marrying and having children are significant factors that enter into the definition of both sexual and gender identities"[1]. Every young man and woman desires to get married and have children. Some women are ready to marry any man available provided they get out of their fathers' house to avoid being made fun of. Some men make their future wives pregnant first in order to make sure that they will conceive before they make arrangements for a Church wedding. They don't want to take any risk that will make them feel useless in their communities.

In this situation, marrying and getting children could be arranged, planned, or simply entered into because one is up to the age. The more personal dimension of relationship is generally overlooked or implicitly considered of secondary importance. Indeed, it is not that important for some because the main object of their marital relationship is to have children and be socially secure. After all, some young women believe that love should be set aside as long as they find someone to marry them. Some men are focused on marrying women who will get children, male and female 'for them'. Whatever happens afterwards should be managed. The problem of marital relationship, however, does truly emerge in most cases when marriage ceremonies have been concluded and children have also arrived. It is then that the issue of love and intimacy become important. Loneliness has set in, but it is not understood for what it is.

In this tacit cultural understanding, people come up with various ways of managing the shadow side of this cultural ideal, such as having illegal 'concubines' in different cities, having lovers outside the marital home; others focus on their children and their original family relationship and put aside their spouse. There are also those who surrender their lives to depression and irritated life. These are methods of dealing with unfulfilling marital relationships. Some people do not even believe anything is wrong with having substitute lovers outside their marriage. When confronted, women involved in this kind of life tend to say: "I have done my duty by giving birth to male and female children. What accusation would anyone lay on me? It would be different and serious if I had not lived up to the reason for my coming into their family. But now, I should enjoy myself rather than living in that hell!" Some men in the same situation will boast of their wives not as their companions, but as making them proud for being mothers of their children. Outside this use, the wives could as well be useless, not up to date, not fashionable, not worthy to be presented in public, should not be told everything about business because they are not good enough; should not be asked for advice. Well, if wives are meant to bear your children, and your wife has done the job, why do you have to slave yourself for her? You should be free to seek advice, rest or enjoyment from whomever you can get it". Such general statements as these express the kind of relationship which some married men expect to exist between them and their wives. For such men, relationship with their wives comes only after their children and their finances. Some believe strongly that if children were not important to maintain one's lineage and social integrity, they would prefer to live freely with as many women as possible, as their need would arise. For this reason, it seems that infidelity among married men is somehow tacitly expected and even sanctioned than infidelity among married women, as if the same act is different for men and for women. Some men claim that they have the right to have extramarital affairs, and "if she does not like it, she can leave for her family!"

It is evident that the cultural ideal of getting married and having children has a stressful shadow side: marital loneliness. While it is a great value to marry and have children, it is equally important that the spouses develop a true and genuine relationship between themselves. This companionship has always been there in the culture, and received more boost from Christianity. However, the desire to get married and have children seems too strong as to overshadow this important aspect. Divorce rates are very low in African-Igbo culture because of the strong value of marriage. But as more married people talk about their experiences in marriage, it is becoming clear that many people suffer in silence. It is not bad will that is at work here; it is just the shadow side of the cultural ideal to get married and have children without due preparation for the challenges involved.

At the age of 24, Chinyere was already worried that she was still in her father's house. Some of her age mates had been married and two of them had children already. Being the oldest girl of her parents, she was more afraid that her younger sister, Rose, might get married before her. Her fear was confirmed shortly after she came back from National Youth Service and started her new job in a bank. The marriage of Rose was unbearable to Chinyere. Eleven months after her wedding Rose gave birth to a bouncing baby boy. Chinyere found herself weighed down by the social status of her younger sister. At the age of 32, she had become desperate without a husband. Her sister Rose was in her fourth pregnancy. Chinyere joined the Charismatic Movement and received all kinds of prayers and deliverances. But Mr. Husband was nowhere to be found. Then approaching her 35th year, Ugochukwu, a struggling businessman offered his hand for marriage to Chinyere. She told him she was going to think about it. But in all honesty, she was trying to fulfil all righteousness, so that people would not laugh at her for accepting immediately. One week after, Ugochukwu received a positive response from Chinyere.

Chinyere was happy that, at last, Ugochukwu had removed the veil of public shame and ridicule hanging over her face for marrying so late. At the same time, she was unhappy that life had treated her badly. She told her friends that if everything were to have happened the way they should, Ugochukwu would not have had the courage to come to her for marriage. But she had to get married otherwise she would not be able to go to public functions; she would be ashamed of herself, and her mother was becoming terribly nasty towards her for letting the family down. From the moment Ugochukwu proposed to Chinyere, these two sets of feelings have been battling in her heart and mind. As she settled in her new home, everything appeared strange and unappealing. But she must stay, for it was her choice, though she would have chosen otherwise. With three children, a husband and a home she calls her own, Chinyere knew her two feet were firmly planted in the society. No one could talk down to her again. Yet, she could not get over the feeling of loneliness that she started having from the very first day she set her feet in Ugochukwu's compound. She was not angry towards Ugochukwu for she appreciated the fact that it was he who freed her from the social shame. But, she could not develop friendship with him. She had thought about the whole situation and prayed over it for many years. At last, she came to the conclusion that there was nothing she could do about it; she had to go on enjoying the social security she got from being married and being a mother. She saw her loneliness as the price she had to pay for being "redeemed" from the state of spinsterhood. "It is hard to have all you want in this life", she reasons. With this kind of reasoning, Chinyere dealt with her loneliness. It did not go away, but she did not deny it.

Under the pressure of this cultural demand to get married and have children, many people get into marriage with little reference to marital relationship. It does happen that after getting married and having children, the couples begin to realize the importance of marital relationship and the loneliness in their lives. The condition of Chinyere is common in our African-Igbo culture, but not many people are able to deal with it in a mature manner like Chinyere tried to do. A lot of people in this condition have ended up in unhealthy relationships and extramarital love affairs. Others have indulged themselves in different forms of infantile religiosity that help them deny the reality of their loneliness. And this is one of the psychological reasons for the increase of prayer houses and prayer ministries in the country.

## *Marriage Induced by Poverty and Disenchantment in Families*

There are persons who get married not because they desired it or they liked the person they married but because of poverty or disenchantment with the condition of their families. Marriages entered into for these reasons are not few in number, and majority of the victims are women. For persons in these conditions, marriage serves as an escape from the frustrating physical and psychological conditions they find themselves. In majority of the cases, however, the resultant effect is loneliness in marriage, and in other instances different forms of abuse are not lacking.

This is a difficult but endemic situation. A family of ten – six girls and four boys – lived in grinding poverty. The parents considered it wise to give their daughters away in marriage to reduce the family expenses. Three of the girls refused to be pushed into marriage. As a punishment, the father sent them away from home and vowed not to feed them until they consented to his command. These girls were still in the secondary school. After one month of moving about from one relative to the other, two of them agreed to go back and bow to their father's desire. He accepted them and praised them for their obedience. They got married. Before they reached the age of 25, they had got five and six children respectively. The youngest of the two girls, Chinasa, was miserable in her marriage to Aaron. From the beginning, she was angry at everything in her new home. Aaron, taking advantage of the condition in which Chinasa became his wife, insulted her, reminding her constantly that she had no alternative than to marry him. When her last child entered into the secondary school, Chinasa decided to get back to school and get her basic certificate. She did succeed. She got into illicit relationship with one man who promised to train her in the university as a part time student. Aaron himself did not finish his secondary school. As each day went, Chinasa became convinced she made right decisions. At the same time, she could not repress the feeling of guilt for being unfaithful to her husband. She was caught in an emotional dilemma. One day, she vented her anger and frustration on her husband and shouted on him for bringing him into this "unholy" marriage. Aaron simply told her that she was out of her mind. She rarely visited her maternal home in protest against her father's treatment to her. Unable to reconcile these aspects of her life, she literally closed her ears to all gossip, and lived a wayward life with this man who sponsored her education. Despite all this, her life was lonely and miserable. Her other sister, Chidiogo, resigned herself to fate, and concentrated all her attention in her children and in her religion. Her silent tears were offered to God, she said, for the conversion of her father! This attitude did not take away her loneliness, but it helped to lessen the burden.

In another situation, Lucy could not stand the constant criticism she receives from her mother. She is the second child of her parents. Her mother was all over her, checking on her, and monitoring everywhere she went and all she did. At the age of 26, her mother still treated her like a three-year old girl. She had cried many times and complained to her father who usually took sides with his wife. She felt distrusted by her parents and not allowed to grow up. She believed that she needed to get married and "leave this hell for them". In the midst of this situation, Tunde showed up during her National Youth Service and proposed to marry her. Without giving it a second thought, all that Lucy knew was that God had answered her prayers. Her parents refused her marriage to Tunde, but she vowed to live with him whether they blessed her or not. At the end, her parents reluctantly gave in and she went to live with Tunde. It was such an abusive marriage because Tunde almost treated her as a slave, and she had no courage to talk to her parents about her situation. Her marital life was full of sorrows which only herself bore. By the time she was in her second pregnancy, Tunde had two girlfriends in town and he brought them home without apologies. After persistently fighting against it, Tunde decided to marry the two girlfriends. The family grew poorer as more children were born into the family. At a point, she could no longer bear the humiliation and abuse. She decided to bear the shame of going back to her parents' house with her last child.

While these two examples might have presented extreme situations, poverty and disenchantment with family situations could induce people into marriages they would otherwise not choose. Some of these marriages eventually turn out to be fulfilling, while many others become places of unnecessary sufferings and loneliness.

## *Giving all Attention to Children*

Children are an important aspect of marriage. But it is an aspect. A great problem arises when married couples focus all their attention on the children and forget each other. Children become the excuse for failing to nurture the relationship between the spouses. The joy of having children, their loveliness and needs, could overwhelm the parents that all their energy and emotions are totally given to the "little angels" God has given to them. Children are gifts from God and parents should be grateful to God for them. However, it should be remembered that the gift of children flows from the mutual self-gift of the spouses to each other. In this sense, children are the fruits of this love that exists between husbands and wives. The love between the spouses is different from the love between parents and their children. The two are different in their objects and dynamics. They both are important and should be respected and nurtured. In certain marriages, unfortunately, when children are born, it would seem that the spousal relationship is dissolved completely leaving only the parent-child relationship. In other cases, the spousal relationship is totally absorbed in the parents' relationship with the children such that the relationship between the parents is rendered irrelevant. If at all it is relevant, it is only in the context of the service it renders to the children.

This maladjusted emphasis on children is harmful to the parents, and its long-term effect is marital loneliness. When children are younger, the harm is usually not evident because they keep the parents busy and focused. As the children grow older and face their businesses in the world and leave the parents to themselves, the couples enter into crisis; they find it hard to handle their new reality. When their children get married, the parents are happy, but at the same time, they want still to exercise the same control and power they used to have over them, even on their sons and daughters-in-laws. But this is the effort they make to fill in their loneliness.

Valentine and Azuka have been married for more than twenty eight years. They were friends from their secondary school days. Both came from the same town and village. Though they studied in different universities, their friendship grew every day. Four years after they got out of the university, they got married. People who knew them believed their marriage would be the most loving and happy marriage because they had known each other for so long. Except for some normal periods of misunderstanding, theirs has been a great and fulfilling marriage in the eyes of the public. Their marriage was blessed with three girls and two boys.

They could not be happier! The children absorbed their attention so much that their whole life revolved around the children. After a while, their time together as husband and wife became a kind of distraction to them, especially to Azuka. She believed she was a devoted mother just like her own mother. She did not want the children to suffer; she wanted always to be there for them. On his own side, Valentine did not want his children to lack anything; he wanted to provide for them and make sure they had a good education. He worked hard and provided for his family. They literally spent themselves for their children. But in all these years of "slaving" themselves for their offspring and being proud of their total commitment, they paid less and less attention to each other. It was when their last child went into the boarding school outside the city where they live that it dawned on them that their home was empty without their children. Azuka confessed that when the children were not there, she would not be enthusiastic to return home after school. Valentine himself rationalized that his absence at home was part of his effort to save for his children's future. The rationalization could not last long during the few months their last child was away to the boarding house. Azuka brought one of her nieces to live with them and attend school from their house. In this way, she tried to put aside the loneliness gripping their marital relationship. The niece stayed for a while and was called back by her own mother. Then, every weekend Azuka would visit their child in the boarding school. The rest of the week, she would come back from school, eat lunch, and go straight to the Church for one activity or another. She hated having to stay with Valentine to talk. Valentine himself always gave excuses that there was something urgent he must attend to. This went on for the first month, and Azuka started complaining of aches all over. She was taken to the hospital but nothing was found to be the cause of the aches. She started taking pain medications. But one day, when she lay in bed wondering how the world had become different for her without the children, Valentine came in. He looked at her, asked her how she was doing, and went to where she was and gave her a warm kiss and embrace. Immediately after he did that, it was like a cloud was lifted from between them. For the first time after many years, Valentine had time to look closely into the eyes of the woman he had loved before and feel the pain she was going through! After many years, Azuka felt the warm embrace of the man she had known for a long time. They sat on that bed and talked for the next five hours, telling their stories of the past, of the children, of how they had forgotten each other, and of the aches, and of the future. The aches went away that same day. The aches and pains came from her feeling of emptiness. She had tried to use other things to fill it up but did not succeed. Valentine and Azuka rediscovered themselves and realized how they had forgotten who they were. Whenever they sponsor any young married couple, they always tell them to have time for each other.

Valentine and Azuka are lucky to have come to the point of rediscovering the preciousness of each other and their relationship as husband and wife. This new experience brought new life and energy to them and set them free from their children and paradoxically, enabled them to be there for their children who have, in the meantime, grown up. They love their children very much and still do everything for them, but they are no longer alarmed when they go back to school. She is no longer driven to visit on every weekend or belong to five societies in the Church. Valentine realizes how many lies he had told himself and how far he had pretended he was working so hard to provide for his family. The work he does frees him and gives him joy, as he looks forward every day to going home and meeting his wife, his greatest friend on earth.

Not many couples are as lucky as Azuka and Valentine. There are couples who do not have great relationship and literally *use* their children for their spousal needs. But this cannot fully remove the feeling of loneliness in their lives. The reason is because the fulfilment parents derive from their children as parents is different from the one they derive as spouses in the marriage relationship. Whenever spouses neglect their own relationship and focus all their attention and energy on the children, they should not be surprised if they feel lonely despite the joy the children bring to them.

## The Agony and Loneliness of Being Childless

Another shadow side of our culture that is so oppressive is the intolerance of our society towards childlessness in marriage. The agony and loneliness that come from childlessness is beyond any imagination; it is more painful than any form of physical injury. Childless couples appear to some people as outcasts, misfits, people who are wastes on the face of the earth. Even with the possibility of adoption that is becoming increasingly accepted in our African-Igbo culture, childless couples still carry the social scar that something is missing in their social standing. If virility and fertility constitute significant aspects of self-esteem in our culture, it is understandable why childlessness would inflict a terrible wound in the self-perception of the couples. It is for this reason that some people feel it is better to remain single than to marry and not have children. Such a condition offers itself to harsh gossip and side talks that can be very painful to the couples concerned.

In a culture that places a lot of value on blood lineage, people boast of their own children and dream of the care they will receive from them. It is simple to see in such a culture how childlessness could bring a lot of emotional pain and loneliness. It also happens that even when childless couples adopt children, the loneliness does not easily go away, because, at one time or the other, people carelessly throw words at them reminding them that the children they have are not theirs.

In a situation where a marital relationship is not strong, childlessness easily breaks up such a marriage. Theoretically, this is not difficult to comprehend. If having children is the sole reason to get married, a childless marriage is no marriage; if the value of marriage is dependent on the presence of children, then that value is gone if children are not there. In the language of Ernest Becker, children could be seen as symbols of immortality in the African-Igbo culture. This is the reason why "all sorts of marriages and unions (polygamy, *nnuikwa* = woman-heir-single-parent, *nwanyi ilu nwanyi* = woman-woman marriage, husband-helper, etc) are allowed"[2] in certain areas of Igboland. In some cases, an impotent man arranges with his fertile wife to be impregnated by another man, setting morality and the union of the couples aside. It is harder to handle the case of a woman with difficulty to conceive. This is one of the greatest challenges that face Christians in Africa. It is a psychological weak point of our culture that is exploited daily by false prophets and healers who deceive people into believing that their problem of childlessness has been taken care of by God. Many have been deceived and many will still be deceived unless a powerful shift happens in the cultural understanding of marriage.

Children are gifts from God and also they insure the survival of society[3]. However, it assumes an absolute place in the social and psychological life of the Igbo people. To be able to withstand the cultural shame that comes from childlessness, the couple would need to undergo serious change in their understanding of marriage and the place of children in it. First, if marital relationship is considered an integral aspect of marriage, then children should be seen and accepted as gifts of God. The love and friendship between husband and wife is a strong foundation for a long-lasting and fulfilling marital relationship. Husbands and wives should deepen this relationship daily through mutual exchange of gifts of themselves, genuine presence to each other as true friends and source of strength and clarity in times of weakness and confusion. As years pass, friendly couples should be able to feel their oneness as their defensive self-protectiveness shrinks away, making room for deeper knowledge of each other and greater freedom. It will become clear to couples that marital companionship is a valid good in itself, and should be cultivated, nurtured and conserved.

Secondly, if something happens that it becomes biologically impossible for children to be born of that marriage despite the intention and desire for them, adoption is a veritable option. In order to love the adopted children as one's own children and develop that affection and bonding that should exist between parents and children, couples also need to undergo another mental shift to broaden their understanding of children. The emphasis on blood lineage tends to promote selfishness and a narcissistic tendency that expresses some feeling of omnipotence. You hear some men brag about how they are so potent as to be able to produce boys and girls; and women boast of their ability to give birth to male and female. This kind of mindset and attitude prevent people from being compassionate and understanding towards the condition of other persons. Most importantly, it makes them lose the sense of gratitude, that children are gifts from God, and should be received in gratitude. An attitude of gratitude towards children frees couples to accept children whether they come from them or from other parents. Again, attachment to blood lineage leads to the exclusion of other persons as persons, as children of God. Some people refer to adopted children as "children who have been bought". This is both demeaning to the children and the adoptive parents. Others are afraid of the adopted children, saying that "you don't know whether parents have bad blood". Though this statement expresses fear of the unknown genetic inheritance, some kind of arrogance and disregard for the childless couples could also underlie statements like this. Oftentimes, these people who make such demeaning remarks could be rogues and delinquents that would need some bit of sanitization of their own blood lineage. But these beliefs and attitudes reveal how deeply selfish our culture can be when it comes to having one's own children.

In the current state of our culture, it is still hard for many childless couples to deal with the agony and loneliness of childlessness. Some have been able to undergo these value-changes and are enjoying their freedom in being adoptive parents. But many still are unable to let go of the desire to have children of their own even after menopause. In such persons, the shadow side of the cultural ideals has overcome, and the result is a life of misery. Chikodili is such a person. She has been married for twenty-one years without a child. The husband, Nonso, is a good man who loves her a lot. They love each other well, and are good Christians. They have been to many doctors but the source of their problem could not be identified. She also had secretly visited fortune tellers, and had tried their prescriptions, but children did not come. She could not give up the desire of having her own children. She also refused to adopt children for, according to her, "it means I will not have my own children. How can this happen to me?" she started crying. She reluctantly agreed to her husband's suggestion to adopt two boys and a girl, one after the other from their 23$^{rd}$ year of marriage. Nonso has been making this suggestion from the tenth year of their marriage, but she absolutely rejected the idea. Her husband was good and patient enough to wait for so long until she was ready to agree.

The very day the first child arrived, Chikodili was beside herself. She lost control of herself in tears, cursing the day she was born and her husband for putting "this shame on me". Nonso practically trained the three children with the help of his one sister and cousins. The children grew up to be great and promising young people, but Chikodili could not derive fulfilment from them. Despite the joy the children brought to the family and the love of her husband, Chikodili remained miserable, unable to let go of the desire for her own blood children. At 59 she fell into serious depression and died from it one year after. Shadows have the power to suck out life from their victims, and Chikodili is one of them.

### "Leave Your Father's House": Husbands and Wives who do not truly leave

We live in a communitarian society where our lives are intertwined with the lives of others. Though marriage is contracted by two persons, a man and a

75

woman, the involvement of relatives, members of the kindred, and the two families can make the spousal relationship hard to establish and maintain. The families of the spouses can so influence the couple in such a way as to destabilize the new family. When the influence is so strong that the husband or the wife is unable *to leave* their families and *join with* their spouses, then the marital relationship will be problematic. This is one of the sources of marital loneliness.

The communitarian life of Africans is helpful in many ways, but also could constitute a serious problem for some especially when it comes to the kind of negative impacts it can exert on certain marriages. A lot of married couples are able to negotiate the dynamic relationship between spouses and the relationships between the spouses and other members of the family and relatives. But there are husbands and wives who are unable to handle these two-way relationships to the extent that they never succeed in leaving their father's houses. To leave one's original family is not simply a physical relocation into another family (in the case of a married woman) or in one's own constructed home (in the case of a married man). There is no difficulty in making such physical moves. The fundamental problem is a psychological 'leaving' of one's original family to join with one's wife or husband to constitute a new home and family. This psychological movement involves some degree of emotional detachment from one's family and relatives in order to permit one to start a new relationship with one's wife or husband and children. Without this psychological detachment, it often happen that such persons invest most of their emotions in their original families, and keep minimal emotions for their spouses and new home. When strong emotional ties with one's parents and brothers and sisters take upper hand, it obstructs the development of a true spousal relationship. Marital loneliness is usually the result. Unfortunately, couples in this difficulty hardly confront their isolation because they have emotional support from their own relatives. Yet, if they make effort to be honest with themselves, they will realize that something is not going well in their new family.

Since Ernest married Augusta, it has been a war between their original families. Augusta constantly accuses Ernest of not liking her parents, of being jealous of her brothers and sisters, of being too inquisitive of the things she gives to her family members, of not being interested in the affairs of her original family. On his own part, Ernest behaves as if his wife Augusta is a visitor in his own father's house. He is always on the back of Augusta that she does not pay attention to his mother, that she confides in her own parents and brothers and sisters more than in his parents. On one occasion, he told her that her very first duty was to his own mother and not to him. Augusta had complained on several occasions that she was his wife and not a maid to his parents. By this observation, he felt that Augusta had insulted his parents, and was determined to make her life miserable. He treated her like a second-class visitor in his father's house. The situation gave Augusta more excuses to strengthen her emotional attachment to her parents and brothers and sisters. After ten years of marriage, the only thing that held Ernest and Augusta together was their children. They grew wide apart, without the hope of coming together as husband and wife in a true relationship. Despite the emotional investment in their original families, they both are unhappy and angry most of the time. As we shall explain in detail in the last chapter, the fulfilment in marital relationship is different from the fulfilment couples get in their relationship to their parents and other family members. When husbands and wives don't truly leave their fathers' houses to join with their spouses in an active and psychological manner, the result is usually loneliness.

What is actually at stake here is the fear of losing the security already acquired in one's relationships with parents and family members and relatives. Such persons are unable to take the risk that every change and human growth demands. They prefer to stick to the certainty of their family relationships. For fear of this risk, they may remain immature and unable to bond well with their spouses and build a home of their own with less unnecessary intrusions from relatives. Whenever people choose the comfortable and easy way out of a situation that calls for a change, they lose opportunity for growth and maturity.

# Desires of Personality

## *False Expectations of Marital Relationship*

Everyone entertains certain expectations about his or her life, health, career, profession, relationship, and vocation. As I wrote elsewhere: "A child growing up has certain expectations of his or her adulthood. When one finishes secondary school and is about to enter the university, he or she nurtures certain expectations of what the university promises. Those who are engaged or are getting married fantasize about their future family: the home, the children, the marital life, and so on. Those in relationship expect certain things or attitudes from their friends"[4]. Concrete experiences correct and reshape our expectations, helping us to be more realistic rather than dreamy towards life. But there are people who construct and live in an imaginary world where everything is smooth-sailing and everyone is happy dancing and making merry. Such people find it hard to adjust to the changes that life makes on them. They would want to control life so well as to match their image of a happy world. When life events go contrary to their idea of a happy life, relationship, vocation, marriage, they either deny it or seek other ways to pursue their expectations. This is one of the dangers of false expectation especially in marital relationships.

False expectation is one of the remote or proximate causes of marital loneliness. A young man or woman indulges in false expectation if they hope that marriage would be perpetually an emotional bliss without any problem or difficulty; that their hearts will always be on fire with love; that they would be blessed with healthy, beautiful and intelligent children, male and female, admired and cherished by all; their business will do well most of the time, and people will envy the love between them! You would agree that such a picture of marital life is to be found in an imaginary world; it is not realistic. Yet, some persons expect these to happen in their marital life. There are even some unmarried men and women who have decided the age their daughters and sons would get married. These sons and daughters are yet to be born! This is one of those trips to the fantasy world, and everyone is permitted to take that trip provided it is not confused with the real world.

When young men and women believe that their marriage would be "love without vacation" as one girl put it, then they are in for trouble. Love does not really go on vacation, but it does not always charge the relationship with that romantic ecstasy that characterizes the initial stages of the love relationship. This false expectation can be disastrous because it simply suggests that "the very possibility of love is gone when romantic rapture wears off"[5]. Adamma did not accept this reality in her relationship with Joshua, and she drove herself, her husband, and her family crazy in her persistent efforts to keep the initial romantic glow permanent. Joshua was her first love. They were friends for four years before getting married. Four years into their marital relationship, the dramatic ardour that graced their relationship seemed to have dimmed, but not gone. Adamma could not get it: she would shout at Joshua for being cold and unresponsive, she would complain that their marriage was heading towards an emotional standstill with no thrills and no highs, only lows. The complaint was persistent that Joshua dreaded coming home to meet his Adamma. He could not understand what had come over her. Adamma was frustrated because she had falsely expected an idyllic marriage where romance and ecstasy do not ebb! She was wrong.

The expectations the spouses have about their marriage and about each other are bound to be confronted by the reality of the real world and their own specific idiosyncrasies[6]. Loneliness often sets in when married persons are unable to live in a real world and give up the dream of a marital life where everything goes well all the time, and the romantic glow never dies down. It is in this sense that Letitia Anne Peplau and Daniel Perlman define loneliness as "the emotional response a person has to a perceived discrepancy between expected and achieved levels of social contact"[7]. The discrepancy is usually fuelled by false expectation. Marital commitment in this situation becomes commitment to sentimentality and emotions and not to real persons and real challenges of relationship. This kind of false expectation is at the root of many divorce cases in the developed parts of the world.

Related to this false expectation of eternal romantic bliss is the dream of that one mysterious man or woman "with whom alone we could establish a marital commitment"[8]. There are persons, married and unmarried, who dream of a man or woman with whom they would establish a relationship without pains, troubles, or misunderstanding. When such persons get married, and difficulties emerge, and romantic passion wanes, they feel they have made a terrible mistake; that the loss of passion and the misunderstandings indicate that they had missed that man or woman they had hoped would give them everything they wanted in relationship. For such people, life is lived more in the dream world than in reality. Living constantly in expectation of the eternal romantic man or woman, such persons may never give themselves to any true and human relationship; they are afraid of stability because it might turn out to be the wrong person, and the first indication is misunderstanding or disagreement. If they are already married, they live forever in regret, and mourn over the loss of the romantic man or woman they never met. It is this perpetual waiting without fulfillment that is experienced as loneliness. The fruitless expectation eventually leads to the neglect of marital love or even the active search for that person outside the marital home. This is one of the greatest reasons for marital infidelity. Persons with this kind of attitude tend to overlook the fact that "an actual marital commitment means that one vows to stay faithful to one person, no matter how many others may seem romantically attractive"[9].

At the other extreme of expecting a romantic love without end, is the belief that marriage is only sacrifice and no enjoyment. This false expectation is found mostly among misguided religious persons. In our culture today, the percentage of women with this belief seems higher than that of men. For these persons, marriage is entered into for the sole duty of sacrificing oneself; married life is martyrdom. There is no joy expected except that of being a martyr. For them, this is the meaning of commitment, and they usually invoke religious teachings to back up their opinion. They believe that marriage is a duty to give birth to children and take care of them. Nurturing a marital relationship is considered a nuisance and unnecessary. All gestures of affection such as hugging, teasing, are not considered integral aspects of marital relationships; they are gestures restricted to making love to have children, and outside that circumstance, they are considered to be lust of the flesh. When such spouses end childbearing, then all coming together as husband and wife in a physical and emotional way is forbidden or "offered to God" without mutual deliberation. Underlying this idea of marriage is the belief that everything that has to do with sex is bad and ugly, and they regret the fact that it is the way children come into the world. So, as soon as they are done with bearing children, they wash their hands 'clean' of their husbands or wives and face their God and the children. There would be no problem in such marriages if the spouses shared this same view. But this does not happen in all the cases.

The spouse that does not share this view of marriage generally feels abandoned and lonely. This was the exact situation in which Francis found himself in his marriage to Judith. Judith's family is Christian, and a very devout and ultra-conservative one. Her mother had told her many times that if she desired any man to touch her, she would be giving the devil the chance to take over her body. Secondly, she had also been told that relationships with men were the easiest way evil spirits possessed people; that every 'sweet talk' of men has evil behind it. So, despite being an educated woman, she had lived a life of total guardedness towards men and towards herself. Whenever she caught herself feeling any attraction to any man, she would cast out the devil that was working in her body and heart. When she married at the age of 26, it was not easy for her to sleep with her husband. She was so nervous that she complained of the problem to her mother, who told her that she had to sleep with her husband if she was going to have children; God ordained it to be so! But that is it. Her husband was a stranger in the house, an agent of the devil, who wanted to possess her body sexually. She was so happy when they finally had their last child. Then, she would have nothing to do with the devil; she had passed the test and committed herself completely to God, body and soul, without reference to her husband. But there was no need to consult her husband, for his sexual demands were actually seen as the insinuation of the evil one. Francis tried all he could to get Judith to understand and change her mistaken idea, but she could not give it up. The gap between them widened, and she did not know. All that was important for her was the children and she had to slave herself for them. Then Francis started going out with other women. When Judith heard it, she was angry not so much for the adultery of her husband, but for the fact that he had been completely beaten by the devil. She feared the repercussions at home. And so, the problem continued, and Francis lived like an estranged husband; living with a wife but at the same time living as if he had no wife! Until a priest and Judith's mother intervened, the situation would have gone on till the end of their lives.

Healing the friction and loneliness that come from these opposing views about marital commitment would need a deeper understanding of the meaning and relevant aspects of marital relationships. This is what the priest tried to help Judith and her mother do, before he referred them to someone with more professional training. Stories of this kind seem strange in our modern times; yet, they happen in our intensely religious communities with different religious teachings that tend to confuse people[10].

## *Desires and Ambitions that Undermine Marital Priorities*

The story of Diana, the Princess of Wales and her marriage to Charles, the Prince of Wales, illustrates powerfully how desires and ambitions could undermine marital priorities. It would seem that Diana cared less about Charles' love for her until towards their wedding. Her desire and ambition to be the Princess and the future Queen of England, her enjoyment of the popularity as the beloved female icon of the media and the most photographed woman in the world, seemed to have captivated her consciousness powerfully that the priority of Charles' love for her was undermined or overlooked. One could say that when it had become clear to her she would be the Princess, the fundamental desire for Charles' love emerged and occupied her mind fully and never to let her go. She could not get that love, which was so fundamental for the success of their marriage, and eventually their marriage crumbled.

Some people get obsessed with particular desires and ambitions that undermine the important values that make marriage and relationships last. If one places social prestige, public image, financial security, and other kinds of securities, over and above the security of mutual respect, mutual appreciation for each other, mutual love and companionship that marital relationship demands, that marriage may find it hard to withstand troubled times. This companionship is more than the ephemeral sentiments and emotions that flood the relationship at its romantic stage; it is the companionship of friendship, understanding, knowledge and growth through mutual self-disclosure and self-giving to each other that provide the solid ground upon which enduring marital relationship is founded. When money, passing pleasure, prestige, popularity and even beauty, become primary determinants of marital relationship, then the foundation is shaky. These things do not constitute the essence of marital intimacy, as we shall see in the last chapter. This is why celebrity marriages hardly last. But it also happens more often than can be imagined among non-celebrities like Dora and her husband Chinedu.

Dora, a young woman from a poor family decided she was going to marry a rich man, whether he loves her or not. She said she was tired of poverty, and would not fool herself or let her family down by marrying a poor man. She graduated from Law School and married Chinedu, a drop out from Junior Secondary School. Chinedu is a business magnet, with strings of businesses around and beyond the country. Dora's friends warned her that it was not going to be easy for her since there was little sign that the man really liked her. On the other hand, Chinedu boasted he was going to marry an educated woman to show his friends that "with money you can marry any woman you want", he said. They got married and had a high society wedding that was the talk of the town. She was in her first pregnancy when it started getting clear to her that she could not get along with her husband; they simply could not understand each other. Any comment she made, he would understand it as a slight on his personality. Dora complained to her friends who advised her to be very affectionate to him and give him pet names. Then one day, he came home from business and called her from the gate and Dora responded affectionately, "Honey, I'm coming in a minute". Chinedu became furious, and shouted that he could not tolerate being insulted by being called *mmanụ añụ*, the honey that bees make! This was the last incident that drove Dora crazy, and she felt the situation was becoming hopeless and she herself was feeling helpless. She was becoming increasingly lonely and irritated, and Chinedu was also feeling alienated from and unnecessarily aggressive towards his wife.

Dora had thought that money would be everything in marriage, and Chinedu believed that it was enough to marry an educated woman to brag before his friends. It only took them not more than one year after they had settled down to live as husband and wife to realize that though these were important, they could not be the most important values that hold a marital relationship together. The healing of their marital loneliness would demand a kind of shift in their desires and ambitions in order to refocus on the foundational values of an enduring marital relationship.

Njideka also was fascinated with John, the popular guy whose academic ability would not be denied. John was a highly intelligent man, respected for that. He had distinction in all his education. He was offered a teaching job in the university where Njideka was studying to be a teacher. John himself was teaching and doing his doctorate degree. His academic excellence was known among the students and teachers in the department and in the faculty. When John made a passing remark about Njideka during one of his lectures, Njideka interpreted it as a gesture of friendship. She started making herself 'seen' by John. Already, she was enjoying the popularity among the students that she was lucky to be liked by such an intelligent and popular guy. From the day she felt John liked her, Njide became very confident and physically attractive, and her fellow students recognized this change. She basked in the popularity of John. For the three years that

Njideka remained in the school, John had asked her out only once. The rest of the time, he was busy with his books and conferences. John is a shy and introverted person, almost a recluse whose only source of peace was his books. But Njide did not mind the distance; it was enough for her to glow in the light of the intelligent John. Shortly before she graduated, John proposed marriage to her and she accepted.

The wedding was great. Many people came: university professors, academics, admirers of John, and the friends of Njide who were both happy and jealous. The happiness of Njide as the wife of a young university lecturer did not last long; in fact, it lasted for a few months. Njide was practically by herself all the time. Even at home, they ate in silence most of the time, because John would not talk, and he saw Njide's constant talking as a nuisance. The quicker he ate his food, the better for him to be freed from the menace of what he considered his wife's talkativeness. If he were to talk at all, it would be about their finance and the politics at the university. When he came home at the end of the day's work, he would spend most of his time in books. Njide had complained so much about the lack of conversation between them, and he told her that he would not waste his time in pastime talks that were of no substantial value. As each day passed, Njide became increasingly lonely, abandoned, and frustrated. She could not wait to deliver her baby, at least, to have a companion at home. When her baby finally came, she heaved a sigh of relief. But the happiness she derived from the baby was different from the one she had expected from her husband. The realization of that emotional distinction made the pain worse. She felt lost, and unredeemable. She had complained to some of her friends who were so surprised at the situation. Indeed, Njide had to find a way of coping with the loneliness and silence of her home because she became convinced every day that the battle to get her husband to engage in a deeper relationship with her was a lost one. She felt guilty for being impulsive in her decision to marry him. She married intelligence and popularity, and discovered that these would not substitute for the relationship between her and John.

There are infinite possibilities in these kinds of marriage. In the majority of cases, the end is always frustration and loneliness, unless the spouses change their original desires and ambitions and direct their attention to the persons they live with. We shall discuss this issue in detail in the next chapter.

### Psychological Issues: Low Self-Esteem, Co-Dependency and Counter-Dependency

Self-esteem is a significant factor in personality that disposes people to experience loneliness intensely or less intensely. That is to say, the extent of the effect loneliness has on people seems related to their self-esteem. There are many documented researches that show that low self-esteem is positively related to loneliness in adolescents and adults. For instance, in their study of 156 adolescents concerning the "correlates of loneliness" Diane Brage Hudson and her colleagues found a significant relationship between low self-esteem and loneliness[11]. Similar findings were made in another research conducted among adolescent mothers[12]. There are some feelings of loneliness that could be described as stubborn in the sense that they go back to the experiences in childhood. For instance, persons whose parents died when they were too young or children who did not receive warmth or emotional support in growing up tend to suffer chronic loneliness in their lives as adults. Feelings of rejection early in life, abandonment and isolation by parents or significant persons could affect children negatively in the formation of intimate relationships as adults. Loneliness rooted in these childhood experiences would need serious work to overcome.

We all start our lives depending on others for our various needs: food, warmth, affection, protection, etc. Our dependence on others will never go away because no person is an island. However, as we grow, we develop a sense of personal autonomy which enables us to be dependent on and independent from others as occasion arises. Most importantly, a clear sense of personal identity is a prerequisite for being able to enter into intimate relationships. Intimacy is the "capacity to commit oneself to concrete affiliations and partnerships and to develop the ethical strength to abide by such commitments, even though they may call for significant sacrifices and compromises"[13]. When a person does not have a clear sense of personal identity, such a person feels insecure within him or herself and, it is likely that such a person will exhibit one of the two extremes of behaviour towards intimate relationships. First, a person who feels insecure in his or her identity may seek intimacy through fusion; that is, losing oneself in a relationship in such a way that the *self* is completely lost in the *other*. Such a person hardly is able to think about him or herself without the *other* or *others* who must take care of him or her. Persons like this are constantly in need of compliments, validations, approval, direction, and support from others to be able to live. In the same way they are very sensitive to real or imagined signs of rejection. In many instances, dependent persons tend to enter co-dependent relationships. Secondly, some persons with insecure identities tend to run away from intimacy as a way of protecting their insecure selves from being swallowed or overwhelmed by others. Such persons exhibit "counter-dependency"[14] behaviours which are generally designed to isolate themselves from others or avoid close contacts with people.

Whether people are co-dependent or counter-dependent, their deep psychological problem lies in their feeling of insecurity which makes it difficult for them to manage the challenges of intimacy. While co-dependent persons tend to cling to others, act weak and are addicted to people, counter-dependent persons push others away and avoid intimacy and closeness.[15] Both groups of persons battle with loneliness. Though co-dependent persons appear to be very close to each other, their closeness smothers and suffocates them so that they are profoundly lonely because the enmeshed situation does not allow them the kind of freedom that genuine intimacy gives. On the other hand, counter-dependent persons exhibit artificial pride and unruffled poise indicating that they do not need others. Yet, they are lonely because they lack genuine and affective connection with persons. That is why they tend to keep themselves busy with work, hobbies, recreation, sports, and those activities where closeness with people is minimized[16]. Sometimes, also they get into different forms of addiction such as drinking and solitary sex or smoking in order to take away their loneliness.

There are times when couples make effort to get connected to each other at a deep level but their efforts seem fruitless. It may likely be that one of these psychological issues is at stake, and unless it is identified and necessary help sought, the problem may linger, resulting in further estrangement of the couples from each other.

## Breakdown of an Original Relational System

Every relationship is unique. Every couple is different from others. There are certain explicit and implicit factors that come into the establishment of a particular relational system that guides each spousal relationship. For instance, a dependent woman may marry a highly controlling man. They will feed each other's need for dependency and control. This relational system will work for a while unless the spouses do not grow in their humanity and relationship. If growth takes place, there always comes a time when this particular relational system undergoes a change because it has become suffocating or 'too narrow'. "At some point in life" writes Rabbi Nilton Bonder, "all of us find ourselves in a place that has grown too narrow. Places that once served the purposes of development and growth become constrictive and confining to us"[17]. That time may be ushered in by sickness, loss of business, and any other anomaly in life. When this happens, the system of relationship originally constructed breaks down. The feeling of constriction and restlessness is the first symptom that a change is necessary and in most cases, inevitable. Couples in this situation cannot simply go ahead as if everything is 'business as usual'. The breakdown has to be confronted, and a new relational system has to be constructed on the ruins of the old.

This period of breakdown is a terribly lonely period. Couples could be confused as to what is happening in their relationships. It could also happen that a spouse is ready to confront their outdated relational system and the other is reluctant to do so. This is not easy for both of them. The loneliness of this period could drive the spouses crazy. Yet, it is simply the loneliness of a passing period of death and development, if rightly understood and worked through. Unfortunately, when such breakdown happens, spouses interpret their loneliness as absence of love and passion, and tend to seek for emotional support somewhere else. This move is psychologically damaging because it kills the necessary tension that usually accompanies the death of an unfulfilling relational system and the emergence of a new one. At the same time, spouses in this condition should not be blamed so much for the pain and loneliness of this period could be unbearable to some.

The loneliness of this period of breakdown is made worse by the self-defeating attitudes usually adopted by people caught in this situation. With the analogy of Israelites freed from the narrow condition of Egyptian slavery, and finding themselves between Pharaoh's army and the sea, Nilton Bonder describes the four attitudes we usually exhibit in such situations of breakdown and change[18]. First, is the attitude of those who want to go back to Egypt, those who want to remain in the old relational system that has been outmoded; the second is the attitude of those who want to fight in order to make the narrow space wider. This is what happens when couples in this same situation feel that the best thing they can do is to start eating together or even taking bath together. These are efforts being made to casually avoid facing the big problem of the breakdown. The third is the attitude of those who cast themselves into the sea out of desperation. A despairing spouse in this period feels that nothing will ever make their marriage work, that everything is ruined, and a terrible mistake had been made in the past. Since there is no possible return to the previous constrictive marital relational system, and a new one is not seen or believed to be reachable, the concerned spouse crumbles in despair or runs away from the situation to forge a new relationship outside the marital home. This leads to having affairs or to divorce. In either case, the problem is not confronted and the developmental challenge of this period is also lost. The fourth is the attitude of those who simply pray, which is "a way of attempting to make the new situation into a reproduction of the narrow space"[19].

With prayer, the old relational system appears to be normal again and the feelings of constriction are gone. Nothing has really changed because the change demanded has not been embarked upon. In addition to praying, the Israelites must move forward (Exodus 14.15). This moving forward can be frightening, but it demands enormous trust in God and in the couples themselves, that a new and better relationship will grow out of the ruins of the constricting one they have. In other words, the loneliness of this period of breakdown is temporary, but has to be faced without denial. What the couple in the situation need is a re-ordering of their lives in the light of a new kind of relationship that is not yet. It is this not-yet condition that frightens and makes loneliness of this transition period almost intolerable. If they succeed in grieving over the lost old relationship and wait for the new one as they work through the breakdown, they will surely grow in themselves and in their relationship.

## Gender Factor: Unhealthy Masculinity and Femininity

An important factor that promotes marital loneliness is unhealthy masculinity and femininity. This problem is expressed in the beliefs, attitudes, and actions of men and women who tend to undermine the validity of each sex as different from but oriented to each other in a complimentary fashion. The idea of complimentary relationship between men and women removes all traces of superiority-inferiority between the sexes, and appreciates the indispensability of each for the other. Hildebrand describes well this complimentary difference between the sexes when he said that men and women "are two different expressions of human nature"[20].

There are essential differences between men and women, a difference that is reflected in their physical structure, psychological characteristics, and spiritual sensitivity. In other words, the difference between men and women is fundamentally rooted in their sexual identities as males and females. The physiological difference is obvious, and does not need further elaboration.

Psychologically, men are different from women in their tendencies. It is widely acknowledged that "females are more relationship oriented than males. Males tend to value independence more than females do, while females value connectedness and intimacy more than males do"[21]. This difference should not be taken in an absolute sense as if to say that all females *are* relationship oriented and all males *are not*; the difference is a *tendency*, that is, females tend to be more oriented to relationship than males. This tendency derives again from another more fundamental psychological difference between men and women: "we find in women a unity of personality by the fact that heart, intellect, and temperament are much more interwoven, whereas in man there is a specific capacity to emancipate himself with his intellect from the affective sphere. This unity of the feminine type of human person displays itself also in a greater unity of inner and exterior life, in a unity of style embracing the soul as well as the exterior demeanor"[22]. In other words, women have a greater ability to unify the different aspects of their personality as well as the interior and exterior aspects of their lives while men seem to be dominated by the cognitive distinctions that could alienate the affective aspect of their personality. Women's experience of unity of personality is very helpful in enduring unpredictable and difficult circumstances than men. This could be one of the reasons why the lifespan of women tends to be much longer than that of men. At the same time, the enmeshment that could result from undifferentiated unity between the affective and the cognitive aspects of personality often leads to a lot of pathologies in some women.

Spiritually, women also differ from men in their sensitivity and approach to the divine. It is often generally assumed that women are more religious than men. This is not really true. It is better to say that men and women tend to experience and relate to the divine in different manners. Yet, there are certain feminine and masculine dispositions that are necessary for a mature relationship with God. The feminine mode in religious experience emphasizes receptivity, inclusion, and perceptiveness while the masculine mode tends to be characterized by willfulness, organization, conquest, achievement and expansion. These two aspects are necessary in any genuine and authentic religious life. For a genuine religious life, both the masculine and feminine sexual modes are necessary but the feminine mode is more fundamental because through it, the individual is able to establish a relationship with God by an active surrender of willful ego to the transforming love of God. Gerald May who has been involved in the psychology of mystical life, notes the importance of this letting go of the aggressive assertion of the ego in the development of mystical relationship with the transcendent God. Great religious men and women realize in their own experiences this fundamental receptive disposition towards God. Charles de Foucauld was a rugged scientist, geographer, and explorer. He became a great religious man and religious teacher of the simple life of Jesus of Nazareth. When he writes of how God captured and transformed him, the language again is that of receptivity: "And while you were thus protecting me, time passed, until the moment came when you judged it right to bring me back into the fold. In spite of me, you dissolved all the evil relationships that would have kept me away from you. You even unloosed all those good ties that would have prevented me from returning to the bosom of my family, where you willed that I should find salvation, but which would have prevented me from one day living for you alone"[23]. At the same time, his perseverance, tenacity, firmness of decision, fidelity, personal efforts, and daily risks in the dry heat of Sahara Desert among the Muslims of Morocco express that indefatigable and adventurous masculine spirit. The same thing is present in the life of St. Teresa of Avila, a profoundly religious woman in whom there is a great combination of the feminine receptivity and masculine drive for change and reformation.

David Murrow, the author of *Why Men hate going to Church* insists that men do not go to Church because the values emphasized in the Church are the values of relationship which appeal to women, as if these are foreign to men. He feels that in sanctioning and promoting "safety over risk, stability over change, preservation over expansion, and predictability over adventure,"[24] the Christian Church alienated men from its fold. He does not seem to realize that the essence of the Christian religion is relationship: relationship or communion among the three persons of the Trinity, and communion among all peoples with the Trinitarian God in the Body of Christ, the Church. This relationship is fundamental, and forms the basis of the Church's extensive and risky missionary works that saw to the diffusion of Christian values across the globe. It is on this basis that life-giving evangelization, organization, leadership, stability, and dialogue would take place. Without that basis, it is easy for the Church to fall into the trap of sentimentalism or organizational pathologies.

In the complementary relationship between the two sexes, men and women would enable each other to be themselves and acquire certain dispositions they each need to grow in maturity. Each becomes a gift to the other. In this mutual acceptance of the giftedness of each other, for instance, men could learn to pay attention to their feelings and integrate them well into their personality. In this way, they would be freed from the tendency to experience scattered emotions that have been alienated from the cognitive strivings of achievement and control. In the same manner, men could help women free themselves from the tendency to be emotionally enmeshed. This mutual cooperation is intended in the essential difference between the sexes. When men and women deny or live as if the other sex does not exist or is not valid, their lives can be dangerous, and almost retrogressive: "we can see how men are in danger of becoming coarse, dried out, or depersonalized by their office and profession when they are completely cut off from any contact with the feminine world. And women are in danger of becoming petty, self-centered, hypersensitive when they are completely cut off from all contact with men"[25].

There are two forms of dangers to this mutual enrichment of the sexes, which definitely lead to marital loneliness. The first one that is too common in our heavily patriarchal society is extreme masculinity that tends to dominate and subdue the feminine. It's counterpart is extreme femininity which extols passivity and self-subjugation to the power of men. The other two forms are underdeveloped masculinity typically seen in the attitudes and actions of "mommy's boy", and the conflicted femininity seen in those women who are described as "manly woman". The attitudes and actions that derive from these two forms of unhealthy masculinity and femininity are the sources of so much fierce war of the sexes that gets worse every day. We shall now examine these two groups of men and women and the problems they create in marital relationship.

## Manly man and Spineless Woman

When men and women are unhealthy in their masculinity and femininity the tendency is to misinterpret the differences between them as exaggerated extremes of exclusion, repudiation, manipulation, competition, and intimidation of each other. Then the men who regard themselves as manly men or "he-men" as one man calls them, see themselves as superior to women whom they consider as weak and inferior. Manly men believe that they are strong, rugged, and tough. They should not show any form of emotion even in very painful or joyful situations, otherwise they might feel themselves weak. They guard themselves against real and imagined intimidation by females. They do not believe that men and women are equal. They are highly alert at the least sign of a woman's self-assertion, which they experience as a kind of challenge to their masculine strength. It is like they are at war, a very subtle one, with women and they should always be on their guard.

Many a time this exaggerated show of manliness is an expression of unhealthy masculinity. Such men who are so preoccupied with their manliness are generally insecure in their self-perception as men. Their external demonstrations of masculine power are often a cover up for the anxiety and doubt they feel over their manhood. Thus, they can be touchy and easily provoked to aggression. When they get married, they tend to dominate and control their wives as a way of asserting their strength and preventing any real or imagined humiliation of their insecure masculine ego. They feel that they have the right to make all decisions concerning the family. Their wives belong to them, not as persons in a relationship, but oftentimes as properties bought and paid for. Such men regard expression of personal feelings as a "woman thing", and they believe that they do not need to appraise or compliment their women because such "will make their heads grow big". If at all they compliment their wives, it is from the ivory tower of imposing masculinity down to the weak valley of femininity. Manly men are afraid of their wives, and so, tend to keep distance from them. They do desire true friendship with their wives, but because of their fragile masculine ego, they stiffen up and dread the involvement of their wives in their affairs. If their wives ask questions or make reasonable suggestions on issues, they feel, as the comedian Osuofia said, that they are being "wifed", which means that their wives are now in charge. This sends unpleasant feelings down their spine, because it implies they are weak. So, they keep their wives uninformed about their affairs; they do not tell their wives their plans or seek their opinion about matters that concern the family. In this way, they emotionally control their wives and keep them (the wives) subjected to them. In doing this, however, they deprive their wives and themselves of the value of a true marital relationship; their wives feel lonely and they themselves are lonely too, though they tend to hide it behind their unhealthy masculine power.

Such noisy manly men easily feel intimidated by assertive and educated women. If their women are working and earning higher incomes, they are very uncomfortable because that, for them, is a bad sign of their weakness. Instead of being happy that they have reasonable wives who could share in the burden of the family's finances, they feel threatened in their weak masculinity. Since they believe that the relationship between them and their women is that of a superior and an inferior, any perception of outstanding intelligence, increased social status, recognized ability in their wives, is experienced as intimidation. When this happens, such men intimidate and abuse their wives in various ways: they can shout at their wives, insult them in public, talk down to them, put them down, make fun of their body structure, demand sex from them mechanically without considering their women's sexual readiness. In some extreme cases, these are also accompanied by physical beatings. Sometimes also, such men get into extramarital affairs without apologies to their wives. The central objective of all these actions is always to punish their wives for undermining their authority, their fragile manliness.

If manly men marry women who are mature in their womanhood, there will be constant conflicts. While mature women seek true relationship with their respected husbands, they certainly will be frustrated because they will suffer terrible emotional abuse from their he-husbands. Emotional abuse expresses non-physical behaviours that are "designed to control, intimidate, subjugate, demean, punish, or isolate another person through the use of degradation, humiliation, or fear"[26]. Such behaviours include, for instance, judging and criticizing the spouse, accusing and blaming her, maintaining emotional distance from her, withholding affection or attention from her, making disapproving, contemptuous remarks about her, sulking and pouting, and so on[27]. Manly men are good at these, and in our heavily patriarchal culture, they freely exhibit these actions and attitudes constantly towards their wives. Good natured and mature women in such relationships generally live lives of loneliness, isolation, and abandonment. Though there are no physical beatings, they are emotionally subjugated and frustrated.

But if manly men succeed in marrying "spineless women", there will not be obvious troubles or conflicts. Manly men help "spineless women" to finish up the work of domestication already present in the lives of those women. They are spineless because in all situations and events, these women are passive receivers of everything. Such believe that, as women, they should be told what to do by their husbands all the time, when to do them, how to do them, and be provided with the resources to do them. They panic at having to take charge of an aspect of their lives on their own. If their men are out of sight for too long, they immediately find another strong man to depend on. They are ready to do anything as long as they do not have to be asked to decide anything for themselves or take charge of their lives. They feel hopeless and lost if they are left alone. They are submissive, self-effacing, slavish, and serviceable to their men. In conversation with their husbands, they appear naïve, overly deferential, and without opinions of their own. Their husbands can abuse them provided they are not left alone in the world of uncertainty.

For any man who wants a genuine and mature relationship with a woman, spineless women are a bore, disgusting and energy-sapping. They do not understand relationships and so, do not really care about it. All they know is that they marry to serve their husbands and make them babies. They are terrified by the power of the manly men, and it does not cross their minds to demand to be heard in any issue, including their sexual relationship. If their men demand sex from them, they are pleased, and if not, they are worried that they must have offended them (the men). Their men can demand sex from them anytime, anywhere and anyhow. As humble servants of their master-husbands, they should submit themselves without question, whether it is convenient for them or not. Hence, they produce more children than they can take care of. When they are asked, they wash their hands of any guilt because it is up to the husband to decide when to have sex or not. Their joy is that they are still desirable to their men. There is really little fulfilling relationship but rather there exists a struggle between fragile and lonely masculine and feminine selves engaged in mutual self-manipulation.

The marriage of manly man and spineless woman is sometimes a pathological state that produces a dysfunctional family system. A manly man Stephen married a spineless woman Regina. They have five children, two boys and three girls. Stephen is a businessman known for his roughness and intimidation. Regina is an elementary school teacher. She is a very beautiful woman, but the way she talks and walks will give anyone listening to her the impression that she does not know what she wants in life. Stephen exercises absolute power on his wife and family. He literally does whatever he wants without apology to anyone. Since the family is a little bit above average in income, he lives as if the whole world belongs to him. He barks at his wife, slaps her whenever there is an inflection in her voice. He takes her salary from her and provides her with all she needs or desires. To buy everything for the family even pepper and salt, she has to go to him. Sometimes, when she comes to his office for some money to go to the market, he insults her before the customers about her dressing and appearance. He has about five women in the city and in the village to whom he goes anytime he wants. Some of these women come to his house freely and Regina cannot do anything. Sometimes she feels bad about it, but she is also terrified to say something. At least, she is happy that he has not thrown her out. The material needs of the children are taken care of. But then, the children suffer the trauma of their father's terrifying anger, his constant shouts on their Mom, and the stories of his adulterous life in town. As they grew up, they observed the slavish condition of their mother and almost joined hands to rescue her from their father. They could not succeed because their mother was not sure if she wanted to confront the situation. She wanted peace and the tranquility of a domesticated lifestyle. In this way, Regina and her children walked on eggshells at home, tormented by loneliness and abandonment by their father. But it was the feminine immaturity of Regina that colluded with Stephen's weak masculine ego to bring about the dysfunctional condition of their family.

## Mommy's Boy and Manly Woman

Mommy's boys are men who are unable to be independent from their mothers. In the language of Erich Fromm, such men have been physically separated from their mothers but the psychological umbilical cord that ties them to their mothers has not been severed[28]. They relate to their wives as mothers rather than as wives. In fact, their relationship with their wives is a continuation of their relationship with the internalized image of their mother. They are too dependent and easily collapse into depression if anything happens to their mother-wives. If their wives refuse to "act" as mother to them, they go back to their mother for every decision they make in the family. In doing this, their mothers are given the power and permission to intrude constantly in their affairs, and almost take over the running of their family. In that case, mommy's boys need the confirmation of their mothers to take any major decision. If there is any misunderstanding between the spouses, the judgment of their mothers wins out.

If the wife of a mommy's boy accepts to be the mother, and nurtures the husband as she would nurse her own baby, then there will be no serious disagreement. The dependency agreement is reached, and the woman can exercise domination and control over her husband. She takes all decisions and literally runs the family. Feeling totally in charge of the relationship, she determines the tempo and the mood of the family, and feels her husband under her siege. Despite the power she enjoys, she still feels lonely because she finds it hard to get the care and attention that a mature relationship with her husband would have provided her. Such powerful women seek out stronger men outside their family for emotional relief but still nurture their baby-husbands in a motherly fashion.

When a husband is mommy's boy, it is difficult for him to relate to his wife as a friend or as an equal. This means that mature dialogue, conversation, expression of opinions will be difficult. Friendly relationship is hard to develop with such a husband whether the woman unconsciously accepts to act the mother to him or not. The constant intrusion of the husband's mother tends to mess up their relationship and alienates the woman from her husband. The tendency is for the woman to revert to her original family or seek other avenues for emotional support.

Denis is the second son of his parents but the second to the last of the children. His mother has a looming influence on him, and he would not imagine himself able to do anything without telling his mother about it. Their father had died shortly after the last child, a girl, was born. Denis was the closest to their mother's heart, and he would not do anything that would upset their mother. It was his mother that suggested that he should marry Chioma. From the time of the planning of their wedding, Chioma had started feeling uncomfortable at the intrusive presence of her mother-in-law. She had quarreled with Denis over that before their wedding. All that Denis told her was that his mother was seeking their own good; she did not mean anything bad. After the wedding, the situation did not improve. Denis was giving more time to her mother than he was giving to his wife. He would discuss his business with his mother, and ask his mother about his wife's attitude. And so on. Chioma became frustrated as her relationship with her husband grew worse. She felt lonely, rejected, and abandoned by her husband. One day she asked Denis to make a choice between her and his mother, and Denis became angry towards her for insulting his mother. The case was closed. Chioma stopped making any further effort at improving their marital relationship. He visited her parents and brothers and sisters any time she got the opportunity. Despite this strategy, she still suffered the loneliness of a married woman whose husband is mommy's boy. In some of her quiet moments, she would break down into tears. But, what could she do than to accept the situation, as her mother had advised her.

On the other hand, there are some women who could be described as manly women, meaning that they reject the so-called feminine roles and fight against men as their oppressors. These women tend to be exaggerated feminists who see men as their enemies and competitors and would do anything possible, whether necessary or unnecessary, to put men down in order to show them that they are also strong and assertive. Such women tend to deny the basic physiological and psychological differences between the sexes. Gender roles are generally seen as mere social constructs that are employed to oppress women in different cultures. Relationship with men is generally difficult for such women, and often full of conflicts. The reason is because of the tendency to annul any sexually-based differences in attitudes and actions.

Women like this are rare in our African-Igbo culture, but they are present. Since their reaction to the perceived male-domination makes them take a cautionary and reactionary position towards men, their marriages tend to be too conflicted and in tension most of the time. Sometimes, they unconsciously prefer the mommy's boy who will carry the burden of their anger. They usually succeed if they have a lot of money and social status, which will enable them "buy themselves a husband", as one actress put it. But whether they marry a mommy's boy or a mature man, the deep-seated tendency to annul differences between the genders remains a sore point that generates conflicts and alienation. Their aggressiveness alienates their men and themselves, so that loneliness is a pervasive experience of such women whether married or unmarried, and irrespective of their social status.

## Summary

We have seen many things that could lead to unfulfilling marital relationships. There are cultural factors and the desires of personality that could drive married couples into painful experience of loneliness. This means that one should not enter into marriage impulsively or thoughtlessly without proper reflection, discernment, and prayer. Secondly, it also implies that married people should always grow in self-knowledge and in the knowledge of each other. Such growth enables them deal with the shadow sides of their personalities that generate friction and loneliness in their marriage, and also struggle to change some of their false expectations or wrong motivations. But it is always better to start on a reasonably good note. In the chapter that follows, I shall present those things that are necessary for those preparing to get married.

# IV

## PREPARING FOR MARRIAGE

*The tragedy of marriage and the union of bodies in love is that so many enter into it believing that it is going to be paradise and that their deepest needs will be fulfilled.*
                                                    - Jean Vanier

So much is shrouded in secrecy in our culture in a way that can be harmful to people in relationships, and damaging to marital relationships. Though families make inquiries concerning the prospective husband or wife of their children, those inquiries usually concentrate on the history of the family of origin, the character of the parents, and the nature of their lineage. Inquiries are also made regarding the religious affiliation of the man or woman, their religious background, moral values, and the source of income. The information got from those inquiries is very helpful to the families in deciding on the future of their children. In some cases, the inquiries are not done because it is presumed that the good name of the family suffices for a person to be married from or into that family.

It sometimes happens that the desires of families tend to overshadow the desires of the persons wanting to get married. In those situations, parents simply register their like or dislike for a prospective spouse, and that is it. Their decision is final. In rare cases are the persons asked if they liked the proposed man or woman. Even if such questions are asked, and the person responds negatively, once the parents make up their mind, they try to push their way through. On the other hand, there are cases where the prospective spouses are prevented from getting married because their parents or grandparents or great grandparents fell out in the distant past. In other situations, the parents insist that a son or daughter must marry from their town of origin, and go ahead to make their own suggestions as to whom to marry. The suggestions carry the weight of "you must", and in majority of the cases, children yield to the desires of their parents. Not long, the marriages are in trouble.

For the great social and psychological value placed on getting married and having children, people tend to by-pass the important stage of knowledge of each other before getting married. People find husbands for women and wives for men even *in absentia.* In many cases, couples do not know each other at all before marriage. It is enough that they get married, for after all, marrying and getting children are more important than getting to know each other to a reasonable extent. And this has caused a lot of problems even to the point of discovering certain hidden issues that could lead to separation or annulment. In some cases, it is believed that a prospective husband and wife should not see each other to avoid having sex. While they should not live together before marriage, they should be able to meet sometimes and have some conversation. They should get to know each other in a reasonable way. That is why the Church believes that those who are getting married should be capable of giving their consent. This ability is not only informed by acquired intelligence, but also after due deliberation and discernment.

When members of a particular culture grow, the culture also grows. There are certain aspects of our African-Igbo culture that should be challenged in order to help married people live more happily their marital commitment, reduce the number of invalid marriages, and allow prospective spouses the freedom to be responsible for their choices and decisions. In this chapter, I am suggesting the necessary things that persons preparing to get married should know about themselves and the person they want to marry. In my clinical work with married couples, these seem to be consistently neglected by couples before and after they get married. They are not exhaustive, but could serve as the starting point.

## An Important Question: Why do you want to marry Him or Her?

This is a very personal question that is often not asked. It may seem unnecessary since people believe they know why they want to get married. But I have often been surprised when young people who are getting married could not come up spontaneously with an answer to so simple a question. One good reason why this personal question is necessary is that it helps the person getting married to know that he or she is consciously going into it and not thoughtlessly or by chance. There are people who say that they are getting married because they are of age. This kind of response would sound stupid to any person with common sense because being of age should not be the major reason for getting married. A young woman got angry at me for asking her this question, and she lashed out at me saying: "I'm the last remaining among my friends to get married. Do you think it is funny to remain like this, without a husband of my own?" While I understood that the anger was coming from social pressure, I also tried to convince her that it was necessary to make the marriage a personal decision and choice.

Even if you are under social pressure, it is necessary for you to know and acknowledge that. Like Judith in the last chapter, you should be able to tell yourself that you are marrying this man or that woman because of social pressure. It means you know what you are doing. This personalized knowledge prepares you psychologically to undertake the task of making the marriage work. It is important to be able to have good reasons why you should marry that man or woman, reasons that are genuine and reasonably objective and attractive to you in spite of the social influences.

It happens also that you may desire to marry this person because of money, level of education, beauty, physical structure, their family is rich or popular, or that their family would improve your prestige. The list of why people get married can be endless. Or, a person wants to marry you because of one or two or all of these reasons. It is necessary to know these things the extent that is possible. Marrying for these reasons may not seem to be wrong, but they certainly should not be the major reason for marriage. Money, education, popularity, beauty, and many others like them, are good in themselves and important in relationships, but they may not stand the trials of marital relationships if they constitute the essential reasons for marriage. Hence, purification of intention is important in contemplating marriage. This entails self-examination and self-questioning that will help you become more conscious of the step you are taking and why you are taking it. I remember a young woman who married a very tall and muscular man with the belief that their children would be great, since she came from a family of average-size people. Unfortunately, she suffered much physical abuse from her husband. Though she had beautiful babies, she regretted that marriage till today. A man also married a woman from a rich family with the hope that the family would help him in his business. The woman's family did help him in business, and his income became better. But he had strings of women everywhere who spent his money. In discussion with his friends, he would confess that he actually married his wife for the sake of financial need he had at that time.

These examples, especially the last one, show how painful it can be to give oneself to a marriage that is based so much on utility or just gain. When everything settles down, the heart seeks for the basic object: love and love only! If love is the motivation for marriage, the challenges of life can be handled better even in the absence of money, beauty, health, popularity, and so on. It is the love between the spouses that binds them together, providing them the solid background from which they could grow and mature together, facing the vicissitudes of life together. In loving your future spouse, you affirm his or her intrinsic value as a human person to whom you may offer your whole self, body, soul, and spirit, and be enriched yourself. When these other reasons take the center of a person's heart in marriage, then the seeds for future marital loneliness have been sown.

In our communitarian culture, there are so many marriages that are entered into in order to please parents. It is good to honour and respect one's parents. But in matters like this, it is important to know what you want and to be convinced that what you want is reasonable and meaningful. Some parents often use their children to pursue their private interests. This is an injustice to the children. In the distant past, this could be understood and allowed. In the present circumstances, it is good that parents make their own suggestions to their children and allow them to make their own decision. One consistent reason why some marriages reach the tribunal for annulment today is parental force, especially on women, to marry someone they (the children) have no liking for. Sometimes women are pushed by their parents to marry some men in order to uplift the financial condition of their families. People getting married should do their best to make sure that their decision is theirs to make. Even if you eventually agree to your parents' choice, it is important you accept the fact that the decision is yours.

It is also becoming fashionable now in this period of overzealous religiosity, for some people to delegate the responsibility of making a decision for their marriage to prayer houses and prayer groups. What actually happens in the majority of cases is not discernment but fortune-telling. It is like these prayer groups and healers are approached "to divine" or "foretell" whether a marriage should exist between Mr. X and Miss Y. In doing so, they feel they are seeking God's will. This common practice has led to so many regrets, broken marriages, and loneliness. It is not that it is wrong to pray in such circumstances for the light of God to understand what is good for you and decide on it. It is just that what is sought for is actually "divination", *Igba afa*, in the guise of discernment. An example will help. Luisa belongs to the charismatic movement and is a prayer warrior. Three suitors come to her at the same time. She is confused as to what to do. She does not want to make mistake, and does not want to offend God. So, she takes their picture to the prayer warriors and asks them to pray to God for good choice. After praying for two weeks, they tell her that her husband is Willy. She is surprised because she likes Sunday better. She has no attraction to Willy at all, and feels an immediate repulsion when his name is mentioned. But, according to her, God has spoken, and she has to obey. "They received the word that it was he", she says. Marrying Willy for Luisa is like swallowing a bitter pill. She marries him, but their marriage is a mess. She complains that God is unfair to her; that despite all her efforts and goodness, God has rewarded her with a dumb and ugly Willy. She wonders if she is being punished for any sin she does not know of. The situation does not stop her from remaining religious, but her heart and soul are not in her home; they never were. She keeps her home and her children unclean, as if they are thrust upon her against her wish. She is married but terribly lonely. She, however, blames God for her loneliness. At least, that helps her bear the burden.

People should be able to use all the available means God has given them to discern whether a person is meant for them or not. God has given you the intellect, your emotions, common sense, intuition, to help you come to a reasonable degree of conviction concerning the person you want to marry. It is an insult to God not to use those means. Decision-making is a difficult process. But to seek the words of fortune-tellers in the name of spiritual discernment is to circumvent the normal process of making decisions. Prayer, especially meditation, can help you see clearly what you are trying to do, your motivations, your fears and joys, regarding the choice of a life partner. To give a group of people pictures and ask them to tell you whom to marry irrespective of your feelings and inclinations and deliberations, is simply to give in to the lure of divination. That is not a good way to discern one's partner.

## Know the Person you want to marry

Ifeoma and Stanley have been married for three years, but Stanley has not slept with his wife more than seven times. They have no child. He lives in the North and his wife lives in the West. He visits Ifeoma once after some months. Though newly married and away from his wife, he shows no excitement in seeing his wife each time he comes back. Ifeoma has been wondering about this unusual behaviour. When she makes sexual demands from him, he interprets it that she is being preoccupied with sex. Yet, Ifeoma is worried that she has not been made pregnant. Whenever he is away to the North, some townsmen in the city, especially Stanley's best man, approach Ifeoma to help her get children, but she refuses. This continued for two years, and Ifeoma could not take it anymore. On further inquiry, Ifeoma discovered that Stanley was a homosexual. His long absences were meant to frustrate Ifeoma so that she would meet other men and get pregnant. In this way, he would be able to hide his homosexual orientation and practice and pass for a father. His religious indictment of Ifeoma for being sexually demanding was also a strategy he used to keep her distant from him. Everything was designed to help him get away with his sexual orientation and still pass for a heterosexual man able to father children. By the time Ifeoma came to know this aspect of Stanley, she had been married for seven years without any child. How could she tell the story? If she had known the man she was marrying, she would have been able to find this out on time, or at least, act on her first suspicion. The annulment process took a year and half to be completed, and Ifeoma returned to her father's house at the age of 35, full of bitterness, anger and regret. How did it happen?

Stanley actually told Ifeoma's mother that he wanted to marry her daughter. Ifeoma's mother came from the same village as Stanley. At that time, Ifeoma was working in the western part of the country. The only time Ifeoma met with Stanley was when he came with his people to start the process of marriage. When Ifeoma arrived at Stanley's home after the ceremonies, she had to stay with her mother-in-law. Stanley always gave religious reasons why Ifeoma should stay away from him. She was happy that her husband was not like those men "who are always in a hurry to make their wives pregnant", she said. Ifeoma stayed two days only and left for Akure where she was working. They communicated through the phone. Ifeoma could recollect that their discussions even on the phone lacked excitement. Whenever he told her "I love you", it was cold. At a time, she began to feel that Stanley might not have loved her really, but waved off the feeling, blaming it on the phone and the distance between them. Their discussions on the phone were limited to "how are you", and "how is your work going", and the likes. And it was Ifeoma who called him most of the time. They met again briefly to plan for their wedding, but Ifeoma operated from her own family. Even on the wedding day, Ifeoma felt in her gut that there was something cold about her husband: there was no spontaneity or cheerfulness. Again, she suspected it might be that he was being shy, as some men are during their wedding. She concentrated herself in enjoying her new status as a married woman.

When everything was over that day, they went into their room. She expected a soothing night of peace and rest in the arms of her husband but all she got was a man who laid back towards her complaining that he was exhausted from the day's activities. He woke up the following morning, threw a "good morning" to her, and left the house for a meeting of his Age Grade. Ifeoma was stunned! She picked up the phone and rang her girlfriend, who told her to be patient because the man might be timid, being a very religious person. The second night, she struggled to get attention from him, and they did make love that was also a struggle. After that night, Ifeoma was no longer in doubt that something was wrong with her husband, but she could not tell what it was. Three days after, Stanley left for Maiduguri where he lived, and Ifeoma returned to Akure. Suggestions for both of them to live in the same city were completely rejected by Stanley. Ifeoma could stay three months without seeing her husband. In the meantime, other men were harassing her for sex. Ifeoma then came to be convinced that there was more to this situation than shyness, religious devotion and tiredness. She made the inquiries and finally came to know the real Stanley, her husband. She could not believe herself. She felt ashamed, stupid, and naïve. "I just don't know why I left myself to be lured into this mess. I should have listened to my feelings", she told herself with tears.

After seven years of hopeless marriage, Ifeoma would start again her marital life from scratch. But the shame of the whole incident was so hard for her to get off her face. She was reluctant to get married again. At the same time, she felt the urge to marry so as to see if she could have some peace. She did marry again. This time, she asked the suitor every question on earth except the ones she did not remember. They met many times and talked at length about themselves and told the stories of their lives. She was not ready to make the mistake a second time. Not many people, however, are as lucky as Ifeoma to end their story on a good note.

Since to marry and have children stand in the forefront of marital life in our African-Igbo culture, getting to know each other is often overlooked as an important aspect of the process of forming a lasting marital bond. Ifeoma married a man she did not know. All she knew of him was that he came from her mother's village, and was related to her mother, that he was a business man dealing on timber in Maiduguri, that he was the second son of his parents. Apart from this information, she was quite ignorant of who this human being was with the name Stanley and with whom she planned to settle down in marriage. She finally came to know him in a very hard way. Such lack of knowledge should not be permitted when one is preparing to get married. You should be able to know the person you are marrying. This knowledge has to happen at two levels: the formal and the personal levels.

## *Know the Formal Aspects of the Person*

The first level concerns the more formal knowledge about the person you want to marry: his or her true names, authentic date of birth, age, genotype, medical history, that is whether he or she has any medical problem; level of education, town of origin, religious affiliation, parents, position in family, family constitution, family history, level of education, occupation, level of income, the social status of the family in the town, and so on. This information is readily available on inquiry. There have been instances where some people change the date of their birth to appear younger. A forty-three year old woman changed her date of birth to read she was thirty-three. This was eventually found out, and it led to the annulment of the marriage. There have been cases also where some people falsify their genotype and give birth to children with sickle cell disease. A sterile man went into his second marriage because his wife left him after she found out he was sterile. Yet, the man could not accept his medical condition. This same man who knew his condition married another woman. On inquiry, he told the woman that he did not have any problem, that his wife left him for selfish reasons. He had medical documents to show that he was able to make a woman pregnant. He was proved wrong eventually because he could not make his wife pregnant. Eventually, he had to admit his condition to his wife but pleaded with her not to expose him to the public. He suggested that she should meet another man for children, and he would not care which man she met. The wife agreed and went to her longtime boyfriend who made her pregnant. She had three children from him. So, the townspeople believed that the former wife was responsible for their childlessness. But then, after some time, the husband began to feel uncomfortable with the whole arrangement. In his anger one day, he blew up the whole secret, and his story filtered to the public. He became terrible to live with, and the gossip of the public did not help matters.

With the high rate of corruption in the country today, laboratory technicians, educationists, and even religious workers are often bribed to falsify relevant documents for people who are desperate to get married. Again, this shows how the social status of being married and having children far outweighs other elements of marriage, that people can do anything possible to acquire it. In situations of doubt, the Church takes a definitive stand and demands laboratory results from certified laboratories. This has been helpful in discouraging many bad and regretful marriages.

## *Know the Person more Deeply*

The information obtained at the first level is not enough to know reasonably well the person you want to marry. The formal aspects of the person somehow say a lot but not very much about the person. Persons are unique and different not merely on the basis of their towns of origin, parents, complexion, or level of education; we are deeply unique in our character, attitude, inclinations, values, and general vision of life. You have not known the person you want to marry very well if you don't know the things they like or dislike, what makes them annoyed, what occupies them, what they invest their emotions in, how they react to criticism, to problems, to difficulties, and to joyful events. You have not known the person well if you don't know the moral values that are important to them, the way they understand relationship and marriage: whether they believe in fidelity or not, total commitment or half commitment, and how they feel about you as a person.

In addition to these, you should be able to know the history of the person's relationship: the significant persons in their lives, how they hold their parents and brothers and sisters, their love life, men and women who have made important impacts on their lives and how they are related to them. Has there been a significant relationship with a man or woman before? Did they break up or not? How did the relationship go and why did it end? Or, has it not ended? There was a typical case of Joe and Nancy who loved each other so much. They could not marry each other because the parents of Nancy refused since Joe came from a town they did not quite like. Joe eventually married Stella and Nancy married Bart. Yet, Joe's heart never left Nancy and the same with her. In cases like this, it is important to find out how the person handles this situation. Another example is the story of Arthur and Ify. They were friends from the secondary school and continued to be friends afterwards. When they started planning about getting married, they tested for their genotype and found out that both were AS. They could not marry each other for fear of getting children with SS genotype. They cried over this discovery for weeks. Ify believed that if she did not marry Arthur, her life would be miserable, and so did Arthur. But they had to give up the idea of marrying themselves for the sake of getting healthy children. If you were to meet Arthur or Ify, you should be able to know how they still feel about each other, and how they hope they can develop new relationships with others that would lead to a happy married life. This is the kind of knowledge that should never be taken lightly because there have been cases where the previous relationship continued to weigh heavily on the marital relationship.

A good example that illustrates the excellence of knowing a person deeply is the story of Johnny. Johnny and Eugenia had been good friends for a long time. They knew and loved each other so much that they planned to get married. One week before the marriage ceremonies could start, Eugenia died in a motor accident. It was such a shock to Johnny.

Eugenia's image followed him everywhere he went and in all he did. When he recovered from the shock and started to see Eunice for marriage, he felt she would be a kind of "second wife" to him. One day, as they were conversing, Eunice felt that his mind was somewhere else. She asked him what happened. Johnny lied to her, telling her that he simply remembered an appointment he had with a friend two days before, which he forgot to attend. Eunice believed him. On another day, they were together in the midst of her two girlfriends, when she felt again that Johnny's mind had gone somewhere. After the get-together, and before they could go their ways that day, she insisted that there was something Johnny was hiding from her. Johnny again denied, and gave other excuses. Uncomfortable with the situation, Eunice started withdrawing from him, believing that he was not telling her the truth. Eventually, Johnny told her his story with Eugenia. He was afraid that Eunice would be disappointed and leave him. On the contrary, Eunice was impressed that he could love a woman so intensely and genuinely like that. She empathized with Johnny's situation and consoled him. That gesture of Eunice was the magic that broke through Johnny's desolation and enabled him to develop an equally genuine love for Eunice. They eventually got married and are among the happiest couples I know. And the key is: they know themselves personally.

A very difficult area for people to discuss about themselves is their sexual history. Questions in this area tend to appear too invasive. Yet, if you are going to marry the person in the future, you should be able to have the courage to ask about his or her sexual history. At least, this kind of question should let the two of you know how necessary it is to be open to each other. The story of Ifeoma we narrated in the last section would have been different if she had known Stanley's sexual history; she would have found out that he was a homosexual or, at least, she would have followed her intuition. In this age of HIV, it is important to know whether your prospective spouse is free or not. There should be no shame in discussing matters like this.

Persons preparing to get married should try to be very honest in giving out information concerning themselves. There have been cases where some girls claim to be virgins while in actual fact they are not. When the truth comes out eventually, the mood of the marriage changes completely, and, in most cases, forever. Such girls are afraid that they will lose the opportunity of getting married if they tell the truth. But it is always better to speak and live in the truth than to live in shame when the lie finally comes out. This kind of fact cannot be hidden for long. Some men also deny they have had multiple sexual relationships. There are cases where men had had children outside wedlock and before getting married, and their legitimate wives did not know and did not ask. David is an example. Before he married Franca, he had a daughter with Juliet. After some years in the marriage, Juliet surfaced again in his life with his daughter and demanded both attention and financial assistance. Franca was shocked, but could not do anything. This incident opened up the stories of other women her husband had been sleeping with before and after he married her. The most painful thing in the story was that she did not know her husband that much. In another case, a young woman told her fiancé that she had had sexual intercourse before. Her fiancé did not mind that. But he also asked her if she had ever had an abortion, and she said no; she could not do a horrible thing like that, being a good Catholic. Well, five years after their marriage, there was no child. Medical investigations revealed she had had an abortion in the past which damaged part of her uterus. Only then did she admit that she did it.

How could people who are preparing to get married know each other if they do not see each other and have some time for them to converse? At least, it is during those meetings that they learn to be open to each other and to trust themselves. Marriage is not something one toys with. The idea of getting a woman and locking her up in a convent away from the would-be husband till the wedding day may be well-intentioned, but it backfires in some cases. There was one such incident in which, on the wedding day, the girl discovered that her would-be husband stammered terribly; he could not utter the words of marital consent. It took him ages to verbalize his intention. The girl burst out in tears before everyone. Yet, the marriage proceeded to the end. This kind of incident should not be allowed to happen; it is a great disregard for the dignity of that girl and her right to know who she is marrying.

The importance of knowing well the person you want to marry cannot be denied or neglected without serious consequences, especially in the world of today. You should try to be convinced that you know the person you are marrying, to the extent that is possible before you come to live together as husband and wife. In this way, you accept the responsibility for your marriage. This sense of responsibility prepares you psychologically and spiritually to make it work in spite of the difficulties that may be encountered along the way.

When we know a person well, we also know the values they live by, the vision of life they hold, and certain attitudes they have acquired to live their values and pursue their vision. These are the more enduring qualities in a person, and they constitute the pillars on which a person's life is constructed. To know them is to know the person very well; to know them is to understand a person's tendencies and idiosyncrasies. When people relate to each other at this level, that relationship is very likely to last long. For instance, does the person you want to marry believe in the value of commitment, fidelity, transparency, justice, respect for individuals or is he or she overbearing? Secondly, as Einstein noted, does the person believe that the universe is friendly or dangerous? If a person believes that the universe is friendly, he or she will be able to venture out to trust the world and people. On the other hand, if a person believes that the world is dangerous, it is likely that such a person takes a cautious position towards the world and people; he or she will live in vigilance and suspicion. Thirdly, is the person too concerned with the image he/she has in public more than the one he/she has for himself or at home?

When people are dominated by the impression they make in public, it is very likely they will sacrifice anything to maintain the public image. There have been cases where a husband is not able to feed his family but spends a lot of money in fundraising activities in the Church and in the community in order to keep up his image in public. Persons like that are ruled more by public opinion than their opinion of themselves; they tend to live more in the external world than in the internal world of themselves and their relationship at home.

When you know a person well, you will be able to know whether you share similar values. If you are strikingly dissimilar to the person at this deep level, it will be difficult to establish or maintain a long-lasting and fulfilling relationship with him or her. Friends are connected so deeply in the values they share, their outlook in life, and their belief-systems that are expressed in their attitudes and actions. If you are a woman who believes strongly in the equality and complimentary relationship between men and women, you will find it difficult to establish or sustain a relationship with a man who believes strongly that men are superior to women and therefore should always be right in their decisions. On the other hand, if you are a man who believes that women and men should relate as complimentary partners, it will be very difficult to relate with a woman who believes that all initiative belongs to the man in all situations and at all times! Often times, conflicts between persons in relationships, whether married or unmarried, are simply a clash of different or even opposing value-systems.

## Marriage is for Commitment

It is wonderful to marry a person you love, someone you cherish and for whom you are ready to give your all. However, it is important to know that when people are in love, they tend to idealize their loved one as the perfect man and perfect woman: he is the embodiment of all that she desires in a man, and she is the one and only beloved that captures his idea of womanhood. He is intelligent, robust, handsome, and tough; she is smart, beautiful, elegant, and attractive. But, we have to understand that no one can found a solid life of enduring relationship on the basis of idealized images of the person one is in love with. Idealization does not last long because it is constantly confronted by the realities of human life as well as the idiosyncrasies of our personalities. Time comes when the intelligent man behaves as if he is stupid and lacking in control of his emotions and the smart, elegant woman appears unattractive and almost a nuisance. It is therefore a fallacy to believe that your "perfect" man or woman will always "charge" you up emotionally, so that you are always on top of the world with warm feelings. This kind of disposition does not help you to commit yourself completely and totally to the marital life.

In preparing to marry, you should try to gather all you are and have to commit to the person you want to marry. This implies some adjustments and changes: first, there must be a readjustment in the relationships you had before. It is necessary to assess your emotional attachment to the persons you had related with before you got married, namely family members and friends. Through this assessment, you will realize that you need to withdraw your emotions from certain relationships and invest them in your new commitment. It can be disruptive if you keep your former boyfriend or girlfriend completely at the center of your heart if you are marrying a different person. As long as a reasonable quantity of emotions is invested on your previous relationships, you have given room for serious emotional distraction in your marital relationship. This has had disastrous effects on many marriages. You may not forget a person you have loved in your life, but marital commitment also calls for respect of boundaries and emotional investment on the new relationship. The former relationship should be grieved over and the persons come to terms with the fact that forever they may never live together as husband and wife. The genuine acceptance of this reality frees both parties and enables them to get on with their new commitments with less distraction.

The same also happens in relationships with family members. No matter how deeply you love your parents and brothers and sisters, you must realize that you are primarily committed to your spouse and children. You do not forget your people or abandon them because you got married, but it is important to know that your marriage demands some reasonable freedom from them so as to enable you to focus on your new life in marriage. Often times, emotional attachment to one's family - parents and siblings - does not allow one to commit oneself fully to the marital relationship. Strong attachment to one's family could weaken the heart's capacity to settle completely in the new relationship. This has caused a lot of conflicts in many marriages, leading to accusations and counter-accusations regarding the focus of attention. But the basic problem is that persons who are so attached to their family become emotionally divided in their marital commitment. It is a journey that can be so hard and tedious for many people. That is why it is important to start early to prepare oneself to commit totally.

Secondly, in order to prepare oneself for the marital commitment, it is important to close all avenues or loopholes that will weaken one's decision. In other words, one should make a decision that is absolute and not provisional. Consider these two examples. Genevieve married Kenneth because she felt she would lose her opportunity of getting married if she did not marry him. However, she had it in mind that she would not be stuck to him for the rest of her life, meaning that she would permit herself to receive "fresh air" from outside. She married Kenneth "to fulfill all righteousness". This disposition is an open door, a loophole that weakens her decision to be committed. She will find it extremely hard to invest her energy and emotions on her spouse. The same thing also happened in the marriage of Donatus and Angela. Angela was not as beautiful as Donatus would have wished his wife to be. But he married her because he had reasoned that all her sisters who married had male children in their marriages. So, he primarily married her because of his expectation that Angela would give birth to boys as her sisters did. Whatever his idea of biology, this was his belief. Angela did give him three boys and two girls. Since he married Angela for this reason, he did not feel he should be committed to her fully and totally. He flirted with other women as it pleased him. When his friends confronted him with that, he sarcastically asked them if they would be contented to sleep with Angela the rest of their lives! Such an interior disposition towards marriage already undermines the strength of marital commitment and even impedes the cultivation of it.

Commitment also entails the readiness to grow with the person you marry. This implies the decision to make the marriage work and to improve in your relationships as spouses and as parents. Psychologically, a provisional commitment is dangerous because it leaves the person open to escape from opportunities for growth, especially in difficult moments. Moreover, a provisionally committed person hardly explores alternatives of action when trouble comes. In a word, provisional commitment impoverishes the psychological resources a person has to meet with the challenges of life and relationships. Commitment must be final and total. In this way also, it challenges the persons to grow in their humanity and bring the best out of themselves. Whenever a commitment is provisional or undermined by conscious or subconscious desires, it can wreak disaster in marriage and in the personal lives of the individual. When commitment is final and absolute, it enables the persons to withstand the distractions and temptations that will always come against their marriage.

Marital commitment also calls for a re-adjustment in the priorities previously held. Before marriage, people could do what they liked. After they get married, they should reconsider some of the things they did in the past as bachelors or spinsters and see how they affect positively or negatively their married life. It is good to make money, for instance, in order to take care of oneself, spouse, and children. At the same time, it is necessary to have some time to be together as husband and wife. Money is not everything, and does not solve every problem. Peace and joy have often been sacrificed for the sake of making money and making a name or pursuing one's interests without considering the condition of one's spouse and family. Priorities have to be adjusted in such a way as to facilitate marital commitment. The key issue here is that couples should try to seek the good of each other and please their spouses.

Preparation for marriage should be taken seriously. People should consider that in preparing well for their marriage, they are doing themselves a great good; they are laying good foundation for tomorrow. There are mistakes that could have been avoided if some valid steps were taken during the time one was preparing for marriage. No one succeeds in foreseeing or preventing everything in relationship. But there are incidents that can be foreseen and prevented if right questions are asked and reasonable self-scrutiny is done.

A significant aspect of preparation for marriage is a deeper understanding of the importance of developing and nurturing marital intimacy. This is what people do when they are in courtship. But it should not stop after wedding. Most importantly, the arrival of children should not take the place of the spousal relationship.

# V

## BEYOND HAVING CHILDREN: BUILDING MARITAL INTIMACY

*Weak intimacy acts like a weak immune system and fails to adequately protect couples from outside "viruses" such as job strain, money worries, health problems, and so on.*
- Paul Coleman

Marital relationship is much more than simply getting married and having children. These are intrinsic aspects or elements of marriage. But the relationship between the spouses provides a solid foundation for the health of a family. It is this relationship, this intimacy between the spouses that should be built, cultivated and consolidated every day as a reliable source of life for the spouses and their children. Efforts to recover and rediscover the significant place of spousal intimacy in our culture will pay off especially in reducing the number of unhappy marriages, bad marriages that have been founded on parental coercion or deceit, and different forms of oppression going on in certain marriages many of which are not known. More positively, the appreciation of marital intimacy will bring new life and vigour to married couples in their times of joy and trials. In moments of joy and pain, lonely couples suffer terribly: they are reluctant to share their joys or their sorrows with their spouses. It can be a terrible way of living. In this chapter, I wish to examine the elements that make up intimacy in order to help persons married or about to be married to understand deeply some key elements of intimacy. Perhaps, this chapter may simply perform the function of giving words to what you have been feeling concerning the issue of intimacy in your life.

## Happily Married: the Story of Intimacy and Commitment

For a lot of happily married people, marriage provides the best joy, peace and happiness. The stability and satisfaction they derive from their marriage is a good boost to their mental and physical health. They have been through a lot of troubles and storms in their marriage: financial crisis, sicknesses, deaths, failures, misunderstandings, problems with children, and many other crises. Yet, even in their old age, these couples still radiate graciousness in their lives. They are not simply "stuck" to each other because they have to; they have built their lives through the highs and lows of their experiences and differences and reap the reward of a great relationship that marriage offers. This is the story of Hyacinth and Clementina, his wife.

They have been married for thirty years, and have been through a lot in their lives. First, it was said that Hyacinth's people did not want him to marry Clementina because she came from a greedy and selfish lineage. He insisted and prevailed over his people, and married Clementina. Their first two children, males, died in their childhood. She waited for four years before she was able to get pregnant again. They eventually got four children, two boys and two girls. During the period of childlessness, people made fun of Hyacinth for taking their advice lightly. His kinsmen and women blamed him for marrying Clementina whom they had begun to call all kinds of names. Sometimes, it would seem that the words of his kinsmen were true, and Hyacinth would become aggressive towards his wife. Clementina would cry and tell her husband that the aggression was not really his; that she knew he would not be such a terror towards her. Afterwards, he usually would apologize, and they would reconcile. The uneasiness was always short-lived. There were also times that Clementina would feel depressed for her childless condition and the gossip of people, and Hyacinth would comfort her. Clementina later recalled the day she was too down in spirit that her husband almost kept a vigil for her, making sure that she had some sleep that night. It was the first year after the second child died. During the thirtieth anniversary of their marriage, Hyacinth confessed that he felt he had just married his wife, and Clementina was lost in words as she felt her husband had become through the years the greatest treasure in her life. When they shared their story to people on the day of their anniversary celebration, some people shed tears of joy for them. Some were envious of the great relationship they have, and others related the story to their own experience.

Robert Lauer and Jeanette Lauer have worked hard on the issues of intimacy, marriage and family. They have studied the ingredients of those marriages that do not only last till death, but are also happy ones. They presented thirty-nine factors to the couples involved in their research and asked them to select the ones they considered most important in their experiences as being happily married. Though the wives and husbands filled the questionnaires separately, it was amazing that their first seven responses were exactly the same. The first in their list is that "My spouse is my best friend" and the second is "I like my spouse as a person", and the third is "Marriage is a long-term commitment"[1]. The results of their research have been confirmed by their follow-up research and other similar researches.

It is interesting that the most important factor in these happy and long-lasting marriages is the fact that the spouses like each other. This means "liking the kind of person to whom you are married, appreciating the kind of person that he or she is"[2]. "Liking" is less passionate and emotionally consuming as "loving". Liking a person implies deep appreciation of the person even when the romantic ecstasy is absent. If you do not like your spouse, it is very likely that when the romantic passion wanes or when things go bad, you may not have reason or strength to go on. To like a person is the essence of friendship, and it entails the freedom to be with the person, share one's stories with the person than with any other person. It is actually this "liking the person" that helps sustain the couples' belief that marriage is a life commitment.

From these researches, we could see that the story of happily married couples is actually the story of intimacy intrinsically connected to upholding marital life as a life-long commitment. Lauer and Lauer observe that unhappily married couples tend to be committed to marriage as an institution and their children but not to their spouses. Once those persons are in a marital union they endeavour to make it last whether they are happy or not. Note that the emphasis for this group of people is to make their marriage last. Their commitment is to marriage and not necessarily to the persons who make the marriage namely, themselves! This is why those spouses tend to be very lonely and somehow unable to address their loneliness. Their marriage is intact, but they have little or no relationship. So, they live in the blame game or seek emotional and sexual satisfaction outside their marriage. On the other hand, couples in happy marriages "are committed to marriage and to their spouses. This involves a determination to work through whatever problems might cause dissatisfaction"[3]. Their conclusion is indisputable: "the point is that a long-term and satisfying marriage is not merely a matter of finding just the right person who can make you happy. It is a matter of two people who have some positive factors going for them (such as liking each other and sharing similar values) working together in a committed relationship to achieve a mutually satisfying life"[4]. This is the story of Hyacinth and Clementina, as is the story of many happily married couples.

The central issue here is that intimacy and commitment should be believed in and pursued in any marriage that hopes to be fulfilling and lasting. Intimacy without commitment is actually unrealistic, sentimental and, indeed, irresponsible; marital commitment without intimacy can be a terrible drudgery. But how do we understand marital intimacy and how should it be built and nurtured? We shall address these questions in the next sections.

## Meaning and Nurturing of Intimacy

### *"I-thou" and " We" Relationships*

The starting point for understanding intimacy is to examine the two kinds of relationship in the family: the *I-thou* relationship that exists between the spouses and the *We* relationship which exists between the parents and their children or between the spouses and other persons. In the I-thou relationship, two persons stand before each other as two subjects, I and You: an *I*, Chukwuma stands before *You*, Amaka, and the *I*, Amaka, stands before *You*, Chukwuma. The *I* looks straight into the eyes of the *You*. The You is the object of the I's love and attention and vice versa. In the *We* relationship parents stand before their children as *We* and *them*. They stand by each other and *together* they attend to their children. This distinction comes from Dietrich von Hildebrand and he describes it clearly in these words: "In an *I-thou communion* (relationship), we are, as it were, in front of the other person and we look at each other. In the *we communion* (relationship), on the contrary, we look together with the other person at some object. We rejoice together over something; we accomplish something together. In this situation we are not, as it were, in front of the other person, but rather we stand next to the other person, hand in hand"[5]. This means that *I-thou communion* is specific to spousal love and *we communion* is specific to spouses in relation to their children and other things they do together in life. The two should not be confused and one does not suffice for the other. As the two are different, so is the fulfillment that comes from them. Both constitute essential aspects of a marital life. The *we communion* derives and is rooted in the *I-thou* communion. Marital commitment demands the development and nurturing of these two dimensions of marital love. Deep problems arise when one of these two aspects is either unduly emphasized or subsumed into the other.

A second point to be noted also is the fact that in this *I-thou communion*, the spouse "has become the great theme of my life; I am focused on him (or her)"[6]. The *I* has become the great theme of the life of the *thou* and vice versa. What this means in concrete terms is that the spouses have become for each other the focus of their energy, emotions, and thoughts. Without this focusing, this *gaze* at your spouse as the "sole recipient and object of your passion"[7], it will be hard to develop, nurture, and sustain the *I-thou communion*. It is the consciousness of this fact that your spouse is the great theme of your life that is the foundation upon which intimacy develops. This implies a certain disposition to devote oneself to the nurturing of one's spouse, to his or her total development, fulfillment in the bond of marital relationship. It is when the spouses have genuinely and truly assumed their place in their feelings and consciousness that they experience that liberation from self-centeredness which is a direct result of their mutual gift of each other.

## *Elements of Marital Intimacy*

Marital intimacy, which is the essence of the spousal *I-thou communion*, means total devotion to one's spouse and the constant disposition to give oneself fully to one's spouse. The constituent elements of this gift of oneself to one's spouse are brought out clearly in the five components of intimacy developed by White Kathleen and her colleagues[8]. First, intimacy involves conscious orientation towards the other and to the relationship. This expresses the extent a spouse's thinking, feelings, and actions are focused on the other spouse and on their relationship. Secondly, intimacy includes the willing disposition to care and be concerned for the other. This element means going out of one's way to please one's spouse. The third element deals with the sex life of the spouses, and it has to do with the extent their lovemaking expresses mutuality rather than personal concerns. When there is intimacy, sexual relationship of the couples derives from and nurtures their mutuality. If intimacy is lacking, lovemaking becomes mechanical and almost feels like a kind of violation to the personality of the spouses. Fourthly, the presence of marital intimacy entails that the spouses are committed to each other; their relationship is not casual, provisional or a pastime. Spousal commitment in this sense is more than being together because one has come of age or simply to make one feel good in society. It is a conscious and responsible readiness to give oneself fully and wholly to the good of one's spouse and the marital relationship. Finally, intimacy is measured by the degree and kind of communication existing between the spouses. It includes the extent the spouses are ready to be open to each other, disclose themselves to each other, and listen to each other. Whatever the differences in people's understanding of intimacy, it is universally recognized and accepted that any genuine intimate relationship would include "affection, sharing (including communication), and commitment as part of the core of a satisfying intimate relationship"[9]. Relating to one's spouse in these ways is the practical proof that the spouse has really become the great theme of one's life; he or she has become the best friend or treasure in one's life as the happily married couples testify.

Lauer and Lauer also make an important distinction between "intimacy as a feeling" and "intimacy as a behaviour"[10]. When spouses are committed to each other and share with one another their feelings, stories, experiences, plans, and worries, they are actually involved in intimate behaviour. Intimate behaviour is the soul of intimacy. This can happen even when the passionate feelings of intimacy are not felt. Intimacy as a feeling indicates a feeling of closeness to a person. This feeling may be lost momentarily when one is upset, angry, worried, misunderstood, or when one is preoccupied. Yet, the sharing of these internal experiences with one's spouse, that is, intimate behaviour, nurtures their intimacy. Hence, "in the normal course of life, our intimate feelings and intimate behaviours wax and wane even while intimate relationship is developing in a positive way"[11]. This distinction is very necessary because some people, married and unmarried, tend to equate those momentary absences of passion as indications of lack of love from the other person they are relating with. Underlying this tendency is the false expectation that love must always be "on fire" and never wanes. Feelings can be intense sometimes, and at other times, they can be absent due to certain circumstances. Yet, the relationship grows in maturity as long as the persons involved are committed and open to each other. This point is brought out in the expression of the happily married couples that they "like" their spouses. The word "like" goes deeper than sentimentalism; it expresses profound appreciation even when the passionate feelings are on holiday.

It should be obvious why and how marital intimacy, that *I-thou communion* specific to the spouses, can sustain their lives. It is also clear how the *we communion*, that relationship spouses have with their children, may not be able to give the same kind of satisfaction and challenge that *I-thou communion* gives. The loneliness of married men and women generally reside in the problems of intimacy, in the development and nurturing of this *I-thou communion*. The five components of intimacy reflect the areas in the life of couples that should be given attention so that the quality of their relationships will improve.

Marital intimacy is built and nurtured:

- When the spouses are important to each other, and there is conscious desire for and orientation towards the marital relationship; this means that the spouses truly desire the relationship between them, and also desire and work for it to last for the rest of their lives.
- When the spouses desire and concretely strive to please and care for each other;
- When there is a growing sense of mutuality between them. Selfishness kills relationships. It is very necessary to consider the other's views, opinions, dispositions, and even readiness in certain aspects of the marital life. This is not difficult to understand if your spouse is important to you as a person and as a treasured friend.
- If the spouses have time for themselves, to talk about themselves and their lives together. This personal time should be respected and honoured. As much as

possible, their talking should be as honest as possible, leaving aside temptations to hide personal weaknesses for fear of rejection. It is a very big challenge to couples, especially in our patriarchal culture for a husband and wife to sit together and talk about themselves and their relationship and not about children and money.

## Intimacy and Sex in Marriage

One of the greatest fallacies in relationships is the belief that every sexual intercourse is the expression of intimacy except those done by rapists and pedophiles. In other words, there is no intimate relationship where there is no sexual intercourse. At the same time, experiences of many married couples indicate that sex is ambiguous; it does not necessarily express intimacy between the spouses. Some married people are disgusted with sexual intercourse with their spouses. How do we understand this relationship between intimacy and sex, especially in marital relationship?

The Christian account of creation shows that after God had created all creatures, he realized that Adam was alone. God could not find any helper for him among all His creatures. According to Pope Benedict XVI in his encyclical, *Deus caritas est*, this expresses the fact that man "is somehow incomplete, driven by nature to seek in another the part that can make him whole, the idea that only in communion with the opposite sex can he become 'complete'"[12]. Therefore a man becomes complete when united with a woman and vice versa. For this reason, Adam who is a seeker must abandon his mother and father and find a woman, an Eve; "only together do the two represent complete humanity and become 'one flesh'"[13]. In other words, the attraction between men and women, which is described as *Eros*, is rooted in a primordial yearning for completion. This experience of completeness is possible in marriage whereby a man and a woman become no longer two but 'one flesh'. This 'one flesh' is physical and is often understood as effectuated through sexual intercourse. This implies that we achieve our "complete humanity' only through becoming 'one flesh' with another, a man with a woman and vice versa in the marriage covenant.

It does not seem to me that this 'one flesh' spoken by the Scriptures merely describes the unity of "bodies" in sexual union. Sex is incapable of binding two people together in that unique experience of completeness. If it were able to do so, it would be impossible to commit adultery or even flirt or masturbate. Prostitution and pornography will not be a menace to the world as they are today. The reason why these are possible is because sex can be a mere exercise of our biological capacity. In this sense, it can follow the normal biological rhythm of tension and release that leads to the equilibrium of the biological system. When sex is sought in this manner, then any person can be a potential provider and, sometimes, anything can be used to excite oneself. Such sexual acts are generally detached from the inner being of the persons involved. The sexual heat of pure sex does not pay attention to the face of the sex provider: it can be pornography, children, boys or girls, animals, prostitutes, and so on. In all these varieties of providers of sexual pleasure, the Adam in the person remains lonely, without an Eve with face. In these instances Adam cannot say "this is bone of my bone and flesh of my flesh" (Gen. 2.23), and Eve cannot reply to this recognition of her unique relationship to this Adam because their faces are lost in the universal maleness and femaleness. Hence, people who are driven by sexual pleasure, whether married or unmarried, could be profoundly lonely at the depth of their being because they are not connected to their 'sexual partners' in what makes them unique persons.

Therefore, the expression 'one flesh' cannot simply express sexual union; it is deeper than that. A man and a woman can and do experience this bond of human wholeness or 'complete humanity' when they are in relationship. This relationship is expressed more as a letting go of the usual self-protection and taking the risk of opening oneself up to the other. Existentially, this means a courageous invitation of the other into the very privacy of one's being so that this other knows me in my stories, vulnerabilities, limitations, joys, sorrows, aspirations, values, and meaning. When this *other* knows me this way and accepts me the way I am without throwing me out, he or she has given me myself back in a richer form. My unique beauty is reflected back to me with acceptance. I no longer suffocate in the loneliness of my self-protection.

We can now understand the loneliness of Adam as basically existential and not simply an absence of sex. Adam is lonely because he is stuck in the soliloquy of the self. He needs an-*other* who would be a helper, not only to make children (which could be done even in an unconscious state, as when a woman is made pregnant when she is asleep or drunk), but someone who would help him also come out of the suffocating security of his self. Adam desires union with Eve. It is a union of the heart and the soul. Sexual union *symbolizes* this union of heart and soul which already exists between a man and a woman. At the same time, sex can become a merely bodily activity without the involvement of the soul. In that case, it estranges more than it unites two persons. When it symbolizes this union truly, then sexual desire in human beings achieves its meaning not as "an attraction between objects [but] a dialogue of subjects"[14]. For this reason, marriage may not necessarily bind two people together in the intimacy of their persons though the canonical and civil prescriptions are followed. A man and a woman might get married but remain islands to each other. Yet, they meet sexually and beget children. Sometimes, they are tired of having sex, and their hearts and souls are looking for something deeper, for a union that goes beyond sex.

What actually binds two persons together is intimacy and not sex. Intimacy is basically a psychological and spiritual experience. It is unity of heart and mind. When sex comes into this intimacy, it tends to express this union of heart and mind. In this sense, sexual intercourse in a spousal relationship is sacramental, a physical expression of the bond of heart and mind between the spouses. Thus, the completeness of our humanity which we all yearn for is realized in intimacy.

This line of argument will enable us understand the sexual experiences of certain married people. When intimacy is lacking, the spouses tend to be mechanical and very selfish in their lovemaking. A man may be interested in satisfying himself without considering how the woman feels, and vice versa. The mind is focused on getting the pleasure. In other times, some couples use pornographic materials to get sexual excitement. In these and other related instances, the desire for sexual pleasure seems to take the center of consciousness rather than one's spouse and intimacy with him or her. Some couples believe it is the best way to keep conflicts away and prevent their spouse from having affairs. Unfortunately, these makeshift efforts betray their ignorance of the problem they have. Secondly, these efforts also undermine their ability to work on their intimacy. After all the techniques learned from pornography and the mechanical practicing of those techniques, the couples still live in loneliness. Variety of techniques of sexual intercourse and of sexual partners does not take away marital loneliness.

Intimacy, therefore, remains the heart of marital relationship. It goes beyond having children. Couples should make effort to develop and nurture the spousal relationship, that *I-thou communion* between them, for that is the foundation of their lives. Secondly, when they grow in their relationships, they are spared of many physical and psychological difficulties, and their sex life also improves tremendously.

# Notes

## Chapter I

[1] W.R. Alger (1867). *Solitudes of Nature and of Man or the Loneliness of Human Life*, 2nd edition, Boston, Roberts Brothers, P.35.

[2] R. Chapman (1963). *The Loneliness of Man,* Philadelphia, Fortress Press, P.5.

[3] J.O. Sanders (1988). *Facing Loneliness*, England, Highland Books, P. 25.

[4] R.S. Weiss, *Loneliness: The Experience of Emotional and Social isolation*, in M.A. Carter, "An Existential Perspective on Loneliness", in http://www.parkrudgecenter.org.

[5] C.E. Moustakas (1961). *Loneliness*, New York, Prentice Hall Press, P. 24.

[6] C.E. Moustakas (1972). *Loneliness and Love*, New York, Prentice Hall Press, P. 20.

[7] M.A. Carter, Ibid.

[8] C.E. Moustakas, *Loneliness*, P. 5.

[9] Ibid.

[10] Kierkegaard is a foremost thinker who expresses this fact in a very concrete manner.

[11] A. Godin (1985). *Psychologie des expériences religieuses: La désir et la réalité*. English translation, *The Psychological Dynamics of Religious Experience*. Birmingham, Alabama, Religious Education Press, Pp. 22-52.

[12] M.A. Carter, Ibid.

[13] K.S. Rook (1984). "Research on Social Support, Loneliness and Social Isolation: Towards an Integrated Revew of Personality", *Social Psychology* 5, 209.

[14] J.J.Lynch (1977). *The Broken Heart. The Medical Consequences of Loneliness*, New York, Basic Books, P.13.

[15] Ibid.

[16] Ibid., 99.

[17] Ibid., 102.

[18] Ibid.

[19] A Rokach (1997). "Loneliness and the Effects of Life Changes", *Journal of Psychology*, 131, 292.

[20] Ibid.

[21] C. Campbell-Grossman, S.M. Elek, D.B. Hudson (2000). "Depression, Self-Esteem, Loneliness, and Social Support among Adolescent Mothers Participating in the New Parents Project", *Adolescence* 35, 445.

[22] N. Cruz (1981). *Lonely, but Never Alone*, Grand Rapids, Zondervan Publishing House, P. 28.

[23] Ibid., 25.

[24] A. Rokach (1997), P. 294.

[25] D. Rainey & B. Rainey (1989, 2003). *Staying Close*, Nashville, Thomas Nelson Publishers, P. 82.

**Chapter II**

[1] D. Rainey & B. Rainey (1989, 2003), P. 3.

[2] Ami Rokach (1997), P. 294.

[3] D. Kiley (1989). *Living Together, Feeling Alone. Healing your Hidden Loneliness.* New York, Fawcett Crest, P. 38.

[4] S. Leonard (1985). "Love Stories", *Psychology Today* 28/6, 42.

[5] T. Clayton & P. Craig (2001). *Diana: Story of a Princess.* New York, Atria Books, P. 30.

[6] Ibid., P.32.

[7] Ibid., Pp. 32-33.

[8] Ibid., P. 37.

[9] Ibid., P. 44.

[10] Ibid.

[11] Ibid., P. 59.

[12] Ibid., P. 62.

[13] Ibid., P. 23.

[14] Ibid., P. 62.

[15] Ibid., P. 63.

[16] Ibid., P. 75.

[17] Ibid..

[18] Ibid., P. 79.

[19] Ibid., P. 89.

[20] Ibid., P. 99.

## Chapter III

[1] C.U. Okeke (2006). *The Future of Catholic Priesthood in Igboland. Dangers and Challenges Ahead.* Nimo, Rex Charles and Patricks, P. 152.

[2] M.C. Onyejekwe (2000). "Christian Consecrated Life: the Igbo-African Situation", *Claretianum* 40, 199.

[3] I thank Fr. Lawrence Nwankwo for bringing my attention to this aspect of the value of children in Igboland.

[4] C.U. Okeke (2006), P. 91.

[5] S. Muto & A. van Kaam (1989). *Commitment: Key to Christian Maturity*, New York, Mahwah, Paulist Press, P.85.

[6] See C.U. Okeke (2005). *Love: With or Without Sex?* Nimo, Rex Charles & Patricks, especially chapters 4 & 5.

[7] Quoted by D. Kiley (1989), P. 20.

[8] S. Muto & A. van Kaam (1989), P. 86.

[9] Ibid.

[10] For a clear understanding of the dilemma of Judith, read carefully *Deus Caritas Est*, of Pope Benedict XVI especially Part I; see also my book, *Love: With or Without Sex?*, especially the conclusion.

[11] D.B. Hudson, W. Meredith & J. Woodward (1993). "Correlates of Loneliness among Midwestern Adolescents" *Adolescence* 28/111, 685-686

[12] See D.B. Hudson, S.M. Elek & C. Campbell-Grossman (2000). "Depression, Self-Esteem, Loneliness, and Social Support Among Adolescent Mothers Participating in the New Parents Project", *Adolescence* 35/139, 445.

[13] E.H. Erikson (1950, 1953). *Childhood and Society.* New York, London: W.W. Norton & Company, P. 263.

[14] See J.B. Weinhold & B.K. Weinhold (2004). *Counter-Dependency: The Flight from Intimacy*, 2nd edition, Asheville: CICRCL Press.

[15] Ibid., P. xiv.

[16] Ibid., Pp. 4-5.

[17] N. Bonder (2001). *Our Immoral Soul*, Boston & London, Shambhala, P. 38.

[18] Ibid., P. 39.

[19] Ibid., P. 40.

[20] D. von Hildebrand (1966). *Man and Woman*, Manchester, New Hampshire, Sophia Institute Press, P. 37.

[21] R.H. Lauer & J.C. Lauer (2003, paperback). *Marriage and Family. The Quest for Intimacy*. New York, McGraw-Hill, P. 59.

[22] von Hildebrand, 36.

[23] *The Spiritual Autography of Charles de Foucauld* (2003). ed. By J.F. Six, tans. by J.H. Smith, Maryland, The Word Among Us Press, P. 12.

[24] D. Murrow (2005). *Why Men Hate going to Church*. Nashville, Nelson Books, P. 14.

[25] D. von Hildebrand (1966), P. 37-38.

[26] B. Engel (2002). *The Emotionally Abusive Relationship*. New Jersey, John Wiley & Sons, Pp. 10-11.

[27] Ibid., 11.

[28] E. Fromm (1942, 1991). *Escape From Freedom*. London, New York: Routledge, esp. Ch. II.

**Chapter V**

[1] R.H. Lauer & J.C. Lauer (2003) P. 19.

[2] Ibid.

[3] Ibid.

[4] Ibid., 20.

[5] D. von Hildebrand (1966), P. 39.

[6] Ibid.

[7] R. Scruton (2004). *Death-Devoted Heart: Sex and the Sacred in Wagner's Tristan and Isolde,* Oxford, P. 131. See my book for details: C.U. Okeke (2005), Pp. 52-54.

[8] K.M. White, *et al* (1986). "Intimacy Maturity and Its Correlates in Young Married Couples", *Journal of Personality and Social Psychology* 50, 152-162.

[9] R.H. Lauer & J.C. Lauer (2003). P. 114.

[10] Ibid., 115.

[11] Ibid.

[12] Benedict XVI, Encyclical, *Deus Caritas Est*, 25th December, 2005, n.11.

[13] Ibid.

[14] R. Scruton (2004), P. 140.

Made in the USA
San Bernardino, CA
02 December 2017